Writing Asian Romance Characters

A Romance In A Month How-To Book

Rachelle Ayala

Lovely Hearts Press

>>><<<

>>><<<

Romance In A Month How To Series

Romance In A Month: Guide to Writing a Romance in 30 Days

366 Ways To Know Your Character: A Romance In A Month Daily Writing Workbook

Love Stories: Writing a Romance Novella in Thirty Days or Less

Writing Asian Romance Characters

Dangerous Love: How to Write a Thrilling Romantic Suspense

>>><<<

The single story creates stereotypes. And the problem with stereotypes is not that they are untrue, but that they are incomplete. They make one story become the only story. – Chimamanda Ngozi Adichie

Preface

Have you wanted to enrich your romance novels by including a diverse cast of characters?

Do you want your stories to reflect the society around you?

Are you unsure how to portray Asian characters in a balanced way that does not perpetuate stereotypes?

If so, I can be your mentor and help you develop Asian romantic heroes and heroines that are strong, desirable, talented, and flawed—in other words, well-rounded characters, who, like all romantic heroes and heroines deserve and find a happy ending.

I have experience in this area, having grown up Asian American and have written many romance novels with Asian heroes and heroines. I've also read widely in both literature and fiction areas, as well as taken ethnic studies classes and researched Asian American history. For more detail, please go to the "Who Am I?" chapter near the end.

While I'm not able to represent billions of people, I can be your guide in finding resources to deepen your knowledge while pointing out areas to pay attention.

I will also encourage you to let your characters fly, no matter what their background and to not let fear hold you back when developing your Asian characters.

In this book, I will go over common myths and stereotypes, respectful ways of describing Asian characters, and the tropes to avoid. I'll briefly touch on the history of the various Asian groups in America and point out to you the difference in experience based on when the Asian ancestor immigrated.

Interracial and multicultural romance is a thriving romance market, and I will talk about some of the concerns and opportunities when writing characters who come from different backgrounds.

I will also point out the difference in writing historical Asian fiction versus contemporary romance and romantic suspense with Asian characters. In addition, the Asian American experience will be completely different than that of an Asian Australian. Since my background is in the United States, I will concentrate solely on the immigrant experience to the United States. The important thing is to understand the historical context and circumstances of each wave of immigration and place your character's family in the milieu you choose.

So, come along, brave romance writer, and let's show the world that love truly does conquer all.

Terminology: I'm going to use the terms white, black, Asian, and Hispanic. I know there are objections to each of these terms and in the future, one or more of these may be deemed unacceptable. However, as of this writing, 2020, these are the terms used most frequently in journalism, except for Hispanic where the alternatives, Latino has a gender, and brown is too vague.

Disclaimer: All the opinions in this book are mine only and are meant to give insight into writing romance characters. The writing advice is meant to be helpful and only reflects the scope of my immediate observations. No claims are made about usefulness or anything else. Use at your own risk. Aloha!

Why Write Romance with Asian Characters?

As a writer, you are always writing characters "other" than yourself, and yet, through your muse or subconscious, you are always writing yourself in some way, shape, or form. You may be writing characters of a different gender, different age groups, and different walks of life from your own experience, but you can't help imbuing your own world view and life experiences into your character's personality.

While you desire to expand the types of characters to portray, especially as main characters, you might have been wary of crossing certain racial and cultural lines because you feel you cannot adequately avoid the minefields of writing characters with backgrounds different from your own. You forge on, though, because you want to be true to your characters and also convey their feelings and thoughts in a way that honors where they come from.

I truly respect each and every writer who tackles characters from different backgrounds because I feel it is a necessity to have as many voices to tell the stories of underrepresented characters as possible. The danger of a single story is too evident and results in stereotypes and segmentation—the othering of underrepresented people.

The current marketplace is a messy one, and you'll hear different opinions on whether you as a writer of a certain background can write about characters from other backgrounds. Each of us comes from a unique perspective and carry with us ingrained cultural norms that may or may not be helpful or interpreted properly with the everchanging values of society. Yet, we cannot avoid issues of the historical and current context of both the world at large and the publishing industry in English-speaking countries where fiction and literature are dominated by white heroes and heroines. White cultural values are the default, and white faces are considered mainstream with maybe a smidgen or smattering of nonwhite characters as sidekicks and minor flyby characters.

This was the status quo in the twentieth century, when the biggest literary hits, blockbuster movies, and popular culture were dominated by white producers, writers, and publishers. Thankfully, in the twenty-first century, writers and creative types are making a concerted move to include stories with the marginalized cultures of underrepresented characters and people groups.

Romance, in particular, has been caught in a time warp of homogeneous and "mainstream" characters, populating entire towns, sports teams, secret agent operatives, and fire departments as all white. While many romance authors are motivated to include characters from other backgrounds into their novels, they may be afraid of getting things wrong or they don't want to shake up their fans with a multicultural romance.

You have a choice to make.

You can either continue to write all white communities and you will likely sell well in the time being, or you can embrace the diversity around us and sell into the future to where the audience is going. You can also create the future of romance writing with your voice of inclusion and take the "other" into the "ordinary." Which is the goal, after all, isn't it?

You will be writing into a large and fast-growing emerging market of Asian heritage readers as well as people interested in reading stories with multifaceted characters and settings. Blockbuster hits like *Crazy Rich Asians* and the Oscar-winning South Korean movie, *Parasite,* show that the English-speaking market is not only ready but enthusiastic for Asian heritage stories.

People with Asian heritage encompass a large proportion of the world's population and are the fastest growing immigrant group in the English-speaking world.

In the United States, the Asian population grew 7 percent between 2000 and 2015 (from 11.9 million to 20.4 million), the fastest growth rate of any major racial or ethnic group.

Similarly, Canadians of Asian origin are the largest and fastest growing group, comprising roughly 18 percent of the population. In Australia, Asian Australians are 16 percent of the population, and Australia is the preferred destination for emigrating Hongkongers.

Asian Americans have an estimated 6.2 percent of the total U.S. buying power, roughly $1 trillion, and their buying power has increased 267 percent since 2000, making the Asian American market the fastest-growing minority market in the United States.

Asian Americans are a multifarious group, representing people from many regions. Countries as diverse as India, Pakistan, Vietnam, Georgia, Philippines, China, Maldives, Japan, Nepal, Korea, Uzbekistan, Malaysia, Mongolia, Armenia, and even Afghanistan are included in the category of "Asian."

Many Western/English-speaking cities have significant percentages of residents with Asian backgrounds: Metro Vancouver (43 percent), San Francisco (33 percent), London, England (21 percent),

Metro Toronto (35 percent), Calgary (23 percent) and Sydney, Australia (19 percent).

Asians in Western countries are also increasingly prominent in politics, arts and entertainment, education, business, and popular culture. They hold occupations from farm worker to professional, small business owner to unionized labor, and represent every socioeconomic level.

One glaring area where Asians in Western countries are not represented is the romance novel.

The purpose of this book is to encourage contemporary romance writers to include Asian characters in your romance novels. You might have Asian heritage or you are non-Asian, and you are keenly interested in increasing the representation of Asian characters in your novels.

You are also aware that a multitude of stories and characters defeats the common stereotypes. You enjoy exploring the lives of characters with various outlooks, and you strive to make all of your characters distinct individuals.

You are an ally to racial harmony and put your words where your mouth is. By adding your voice and stories to the mix, you aim to expand the representation of Asian characters to dilute the effects of stereotypes and harmful attitudes toward Asian Americans in the real world.

You might also find yourself writing an Asian character because one of them jumped up and told you he is a hot and hunky Asian man—the most underrepresented hero in today's (2020) English-speaking romance market.

By writing Asian romance characters, you can expand your readership as well as give your existing readers a variety of characters to identify with.

Who is Asian?

More than half of the world's population can trace their cultural heritage to Asia.

In Asia, we do not see ourselves as "Asian." This terminology only came in when people from countries in Asia—a huge continent spanning the Caucasus Mountains in the west to the Pacific Islands in the east—emigrated to countries where they are distinct ethnic minorities.

In today's common usage, an Asian is a person whose ancestors originated in one of the regions of Asia.

Within this vast region, you will have to identify the particular Asian country your character is descended from.

If your character is Japanese American, you would first determine where your character is living and how long he or she has been there.

For example, he could be born in Japan and came to the United States for business. Or he was born in Japan and came as a toddler. In this case, he is *issei* [or first generation, meaning a person who was born in Japan and immigrated]. If he has at least one *issei* parent who immigrated, then he is *nisei* [or second generation]. Japanese Americans count all the way from *sansei* [third generation with at least one *nisei* parent] to *yonsei* [fourth generation] to *gosei* [fifth generation].

Each generation experienced something different in context to the world history at the time the ancestors immigrated. It is important for you to determine which generation your Japanese American character is in, as well as when and where the family arrived. Did they live in Hawaii until the Pearl Harbor bombing? Or were they in California? How did they pass World War II? Or were they recent immigrants within the last ten years.

Do not assume a Chinese American had the same experience a Japanese American had. Make sure your character is an individual by first determining his birth, his family, and his geographical background the same way you would do for any other character you create.

Do your homework on the history of the country of origin as well as the time period when the character's family immigrated.

Also consider the class that your character's family was in. Were they landowners? Imperial scholars? Warriors or laborers?

Later on, I will present some common interview questions for you to develop your character and cover all of the backstory and family bases.

Cultural Heritage and Religion

The peoples of Asia are as various and diverse as any other region of the world. Asia, being a large land mass, is the least isolated region of the world. The continent is populated by people who range from nomadic tribes to highly structured caste systems. Most of the world's major religions have their origins in Asia, and their adherents can be found everywhere.

Trade routes crisscrossed the continent, preceded and followed by military conquerors. From Alexander the Great moving eastward to Genghis Khan forging westward, the populations have been intermixing for thousands of years, resulting in a rich tapestry of cultures and cuisine.

If you are writing a contemporary romance or romantic suspense set in the United States or a Western, English-speaking country, your character is likely bicultural, in the sense of celebrating

Thanksgiving and St. Patrick's Day as well as Chinese New Year and the Autumn Moon Festival.

Don't be surprised that some of your characters do not celebrate any traditionally Asian holidays, do not speak the language, and are generally unaware of the history of their ancestral country.

For many years, people at my job would wish me a happy new year sometime randomly in February when I wasn't aware of the reason. I also had no clue what a mooncake tastes like—even today, I did not go to separate Chinese school, and my family had turkey every Thanksgiving and a Christmas ham. I was more proficient making enchiladas and have never made egg rolls. Only now, after I started writing romance novels, did I figure out how to use a wok—mainly because I wanted to write Asian American romances.

Therefore, even if you do a lot of research on the history and traditions of the country of origin, maybe your character is All American or All Australian and knows the words to "Amazing Grace" and Mother Goose rhymes without any inkling of a popular song or verse of their ancestor's country. I'm drawing a blank on an example, can you tell?

On the other hand, your character could be well immersed in a religion or their cultural traditions. She may be a devotee to a traditional religion or grew up in an ethnic enclave. Her siblings may have different ideas of what it means to be Asian and American. Therefore, be flexible and aware that the immediate environment or neighborhood can have more of an effect on your character than a story or tradition from hundreds of years back.

At the same time, some cultural traditions or superstitions and folk tales run deep; therefore, don't ignore them either.

Asian Immigrant Experience & History

The history and current events of a particular Asian immigrant group is more immediately pertinent to the background of your character than their country of origin.

This is because the local experience forms the backdrop of how your character grew up. A Chinese American whose parents came recently would have an entirely different experience than one whose great-great-grandfather arrived during the California Gold Rush.

It's important to be aware of recent history as well as any background such as the Vietnam War and the populating of Orange County or the Hmong refugees and their history in Minnesota.

Traumatic events, such as the internment of Japanese Americans during World War II can affect the outlook of your characters' grandparents, for example, or explain the lack of farmland and small businesses dating from before that time.

Knowing the dates of the Chinese Exclusion Act can help you not make the mistake of inventing a family who immigrated together during that time period. Also, being aware that many towns in the Old West drove out all their Chinese residents will prevent you from placing your character's family in a place they would not have been welcome.

Do not automatically assume all Chinese American roots spring from Chinatown. During the Gold Rush and afterwards, many Chinese people spread to all areas of the West. At one point, one third of the population of Idaho was Chinese.

"Between 1885 and about 1920, dozens of communities in the West, including towns and counties as far inland as Wyoming and Colorado and cities as large as Seattle and Tacoma, drove out their entire Chinese American populations. ... Chinatowns became the norm for Chinese American life only *after* the Chinese Retreat—about 1884 to 1910." [*Sundown Towns: A Hidden Dimension of American Racism* by James W. Loewen, 2018]

I made a mistake in my *Christmas Creek Series* when I put a Chinese family, the Wings, in a fictional town in Humboldt County going back to the early twentieth century. I'm not going to remove them, of course, since it's a fictional town—that's my excuse, and I explained it as the townspeople defending them against others outside the town. [Footnote: Chinese people actually returned in 1906 after being driven out in 1885.]

More recent events such as the lawsuit against Harvard University's Asian quota or the emergence of Asian American congresspeople add more dimensions to the Asian American experience and can provide opportunities for characterization and plotlines.

Going down to a more personal level are dynamics in neighborhoods. How does it feel to be the only "X" family on your block? Is there tension between more recent immigrants and those whose families have been here for generations?

You can get background material by talking to friends from the groups your character belongs to or reading blogs and autobiographical essays. The best way to get a feel for how your character developed is to get out in the community and experience it.

Since each of us is limited to what we can experience firsthand, we are always soaking in stories, experiences, anecdotes, news articles, essays, and opinion pieces to expand our horizons.

At the end of the day, your character belongs to you, and no one is to say whether you should have made her one way or another.

However, there are stereotypes to consider and overused tropes that you should be aware of. I trust that if you've done your research, especially relating to current events and sentiment, you can easily avoid these pitfalls.

The Need for Sensitivity

Even though the romance genre is viewed as an escape to a happy fictional environment, your reader still lives in the real world. These days, you cannot escape issues of racial tension, accusations of cultural appropriation, canceling of people's opinions, and general unrest dealing with the effects of racism.

While romance authors do not want to inject politics into our stories—never recommended—we do not exist in a cultural vacuum and our words do affect other people, especially our readers and any curious people who might be using your book as "research."

Therefore, we should get things right, make sure we don't knowingly spread stereotypes, and write our characters and settings respectfully.

Changing Reading Audience

The reading audience is composed of people whose social norms are always changing. Demographics shift and so do reading tastes. While I would never use the excuse that something was "okay" back in the 1970s—it wasn't okay, but people didn't recognize the problem—once we realize and agree that a portrayal is problematic, we have a duty to stop using that kind of trope.

For example, non-consensual sex was never okay, but the concept was tolerated in romance novels in the 1970s. Back then, editors and publishers accepted bodice rippers because those types of stories sold. I was not a romance reader back then, but I recently forced myself to read one of those stories for research purposes and it drove me nuts.

While I would never go back and criticize an author who wrote bodice rippers, and you are free to write whatever you want, the market of readers who enjoy that kind of story is disappearing.

The same thing is happening with representation in romances. There is a desire for stories to reflect their communities, and this means a diverse cast of characters in books that are read by all readers, rather than the segregated stories of the past marketed to a certain segment of the reading population.

Historical Boundaries

As much as we might not like it, life for most women a hundred years ago was not one of affirmation, choices, equality, and self-determination. Throughout history and in many places around the world, women were treated like objects. In the best case, they had enlightened fathers who protected them and allowed them to write or speak their mind. However, the average woman's life was barely livable by today's standards.

Historical romances or women's fiction that take place in Asian countries or in the West with early Asian immigrants have to be accurate in describing the sad state of affairs. Women were taught to demur to men, to not look them in the eye, and to not talk back.

I believe it would be hard to write a historical romance where the heroine is suffering from painful bound feet or where she is expected to throw herself on her husband's funeral pyre. It's difficult to enjoy a romantic comedy where the heroine is subjected to the whims of her mother-in-law who held all the cards and power in the relationship. Most of the historical women's fiction written in these time periods are not romantic but tragic.

Asian women fared no better in the New World or in the outback of Australia, if they even made it there. While there are stories of white women who had excellent adventures during the California Gold Rush, most Asian women were imprisoned in the worst type of brothels—isolated by language and customs far away from their families.

Writing a romance in an historical era means you would need to create a very courageous and unusual character who is able to rise above her circumstances. She has to have a special skill that allows her to be fairly independent and able to take care of herself. Maybe she's an excellent archer or great with knives, or she's learned how to mix poisons and is seen as a mystic or fortune-teller.

Study the historical context and familial dynamics that would allow your heroine to learn the skills she needs and show her rebelliousness against the traditions she is expected to adhere to. Pair her with a free-thinking and open-minded hero who sees her as a real person in her own right, and be sure that they respect each other as equals.

One thing to beware of when writing a historical romance set in an Asian country or with an Asian heroine is to avoid the "white savior" trope. This is the one where a white outsider comes in and fixes all of the problems for the local people. The outsider also gains the love of a native woman and defeats the rival who is typically portrayed as one of the oppressive and cruel men of the culture.

While stories with white saviors sold well in the twentieth century, it is not a true representation of an Asian hero or heroine if they or their culture are waiting to be rescued by someone who drops in and fixes everything.

Another thing to watch out for is writing everything from the point of view of the white character—how foreign the place is, how strange the customs are, and how different the people think.

Writing an Asian main character means seeing and feeling through the point of view and lens of his or her cultural background and unique personality. Let your reader pick up the differences in time and place rather than telling them through a white character's interpretations.

Accents and Foreign Words

I have a friend who decided to write a romance from a Southerner's point of view. She wondered if she should end every *-ing* word with *-in'*. Like singin' instead of singing, walkin' instead of walking. We advised her not to do it. Not only would it be tedious, but it would remind readers that she was viewing Southerners as quaint and highlighting their differences.

The same holds true for portraying accents for Asian characters. In old films and books, authors confused the letters *L* and *R* in their portrayals of Asian characters without realizing that it was only a lack of distinction among native Japanese speakers learning English.

They used it indiscriminately in movies depicting Chinese and Korean characters, such as having Chinese restaurant employees singing "fa ra ra ra ra" in the movie, *A Christmas Story*.

Whether applied to Chinese or Japanese or any Asians, phonetically imitating accented speech can be offensive and limiting. It is also bad writing, as you can readily agree with substituting every *-ing* word with *-in'* for Southern speech.

My suggestion is to simply state that a character is speaking with an accent if it makes it hard for the listening character to understand. It's probably okay to use some common shortcuts such as ungrammatical English—but this depends on why you are portraying it.

For sure, a saying like "Bless her dear little heart," from a Southerner has a double meaning, so you will need to include it. Having a white character talk in broken English to an Asian character may also be valid if you're pointing out something about the character.

For example, in my story, *Played by Love*, Ella Kennedy is overly fond of Asian languages and tries to speak broken Korean to Jaden Sloup, a Korean-born but American-raised character. She ends up being rebuked in a funny way when she messes it up.

What you don't want to do is what Mark Twain did, which is to phonetically spell out a character's accent. It is not only a lot of hard work, but it is demeaning, hard to understand, and in these days, viewed as offensive.

What about foreign words or phrases?

The inclusion of foreign words, as they are commonly used, is in my opinion acceptable as they give voice to the character. Common titles are those for mother, father, grandmother, grandfather, and other relatives like uncles and aunts.

If your character is always using *mijo* to refer to a son, then it is okay, since that's the way she speaks. However, be aware of regional differences.

In the Chinese Mandarin dialect, there are many words for grandparents. Some refer to a paternal grandmother *(po po* or *nai nai)*, whereas maternal grandmothers are referred to as (*wai po* or *lao lao*). If your speaker is Cantonese, the pronunciation will be different. I'd say choose one and keep it simple.

For example, in *Black Tied: Sapphire*, the main character always refers to her grandmother as Lao-Lao, and the reader gets used to it.

Foreign phrases can be used judiciously as long as you're aware of the reader's ability to understand. For example, more Western readers can understand or transliterate Spanish than Mandarin Chinese, so adding in a few Spanish phrases will cause less confusion than sprinkling Mandarin phrases.

Some style guides insist that foreign words are italicized wherever they appear, whereas others say that only the first occurrence is italicized. My opinion, in the interest of readability, is that commonly known words such as chow mein and margaritas, are not italicized, whereas likely uncommon words, such as *char-sui* and *horchata* are italicized.

I italicize foreign words and phrases throughout the manuscript, because honestly, I'm not sure the reader will remember if I italicized the first occurrence and then "forgot" to italicize later on. Because of the italicizing throughout the manuscript, it also reminds me NOT to use too many foreign or unfamiliar words as it impacts readability.

This is a matter of opinion, and I feel you have vast jurisdiction over the amount of foreign words and phrases you incorporate into your story. Be aware, however, that if the context is unclear, you should provide a brief translation.

Differences in Opinion

As writers, we are hyperaware of people's feelings, emotions, and opinions. We are constantly making choices for our characters that put them in conflict with other characters.

The same thing happens with the opinions of others to our writing. Whatever direction we choose, there will be readers or critics who dislike your character's actions.

The key to writing a character from a culture you're not familiar with is to write them as real people, fully fleshed out with distinct personalities.

A variety of personality traits, backstory, talents and flaws, likes and dislikes will add richness to your story and avoid the tired tropes that have been overused.

You should write your Asian characters like you write any characters—introverts and extroverts, busybodies and quiet ones, organized and scatterbrained.

Also, don't always make them valedictorians or Chinese restaurant owners or have parents want them to be doctors. For example, my mother doesn't like to go to the doctor, and she didn't want her children to be doctors. Two out of four are doctors and one is married to a doctor. Go figure. Her friends joke that she used reverse psychology.

It's up to you how much your plotline or theme deals with their "Asianness." If you're unsure, back away from a story that centers around a cultural conflict. For example, if you're not familiar with arranged marriages, then don't make that the centerpiece of your story.

Your character can be mostly American in outlook but happens to be Asian, and the plot can be anything you wish. Just because a character is Asian does not mean you should only explore "Asian" issues, especially if you're not prepared for it.

Include only what you know or have researched, and leave the heavier subjects to those who know more.

For example, in *Hidden Under Her Heart*, I included a minor character who is Desi, or South Asian. Because I lived and worked with enough people from the subcontinent, I knew they have many languages and ethnic groups with many individual customs. Some ate meat, others didn't, and some allowed chicken but not beef. While most were Brahmin, there were also many from the second-ranking caste. I overheard attitudes toward the untouchables, and of course, my coworkers or roommates told me funny stories from their childhood.

It wasn't enough for me to write a main character who is Desi, so I left Priya as a nurse who works with my main character.

We can't be everything to everyone, but we can still be inclusive if we know our limits and respect our characters enough to know when not to tackle a deeply emotional topic like arranged marriages, the effects of the internment camp, or the resettlement of refugees after the Vietnam War.

There will always be differences in opinion about who gets to write a character outside of their background, and I'm not here to be the gatekeeper for Asians—far from it!

My opinion is that every character that is not in your autobiography is "foreign" to your experience. I write viewpoint characters who are male without ever having been male. We can't be all things, but what we can do is be true to our characters, which means developing them fully as individuals with a full set of attributes while respecting the culture, gender, class, nationality, or religion they hail from.

In the end, you own your characters, no matter what their backgrounds. Gustave Flaubert (a male writer) was quoted as saying, "Madame Bovary, c'est moi."

Common Stereotypes

Stereotypes are one-dimensional, and you would never write a one-dimensional character, would you?

Stereotypes also exist for a reason. They may be based on fact initially, but have since grown into a generalization. For example, when Chinese people first immigrated during the Gold Rush, they were not allowed onto the goldfields as miners. They then carved out a niche by doing laundry and filtering the gold dust out of the miners' pockets as well as being paid for a service.

Other stereotypes were never true and were based on myth or racist assumptions or idealizations. A common way of dehumanizing a group of people is to either sexualize them or desexualize them. You should never use these types of stereotypes—not even to expand on them.

Finally, stereotypes serve to let the group so categorized know that they don't belong. They are not viewed as three-dimensional human beings but as caricatures.

Since our goal is to create main characters who are Asian, we by definition will not resort to stereotypes.

And yet, we cannot avoid all stereotypes, especially the ones which have some basis in truth. For example, Asian culture emphasizes respect for elders. This is true. However, an individual Asian child could be rebellious and disobedient in contrast to a more compliant sibling. Both are real human beings, but one conforms to the stereotype and the other does not, and neither is "wrong."

Therefore, rather than avoiding all stereotypes, at least the ones based on truth, one way to create a rich and compelling character is to expand on the stereotype. Start with the stereotype and add features to it.

Maybe your character loves his family and respects his parents—nothing wrong with that, but he's also a trailblazer who assembles ad-hoc families with the people he meets in an online video game. He has dual loyalty to both his physical family and his virtual family.

I did this with my character, Carina Chen, in *Whole Latte Love*. She was very goal-oriented and driven to be an investment banker while her love interest, Dylan Jewell, was a free spirit. Her parents were also achievement-oriented [stereotype], but she was also motivated to achieve so she could take care of her mentally disabled brother [adding to the stereotype].

Martial Arts Expert

Go around and ask the average Westerner for an Asian male hero and the most common answer is Bruce Lee or Jackie Chan who are martial arts experts.

There's nothing wrong with being a martial arts expert. It's a perfectly acceptable profession, whether as a teacher, a movie star, or a fight club competitor.

However, if your hero or heroine is a martial arts expert, expand on it. Go into detail of what branch of martial arts she studies and why. Research the philosophy behind it.

Add to it by making her a skateboarder who uses the agility she obtained through martial arts to perform harrowing tricks.

Maybe he is an instructor for Special Ops forces or he moonlights as a jazz pianist. Keep adding to the character until he becomes an interesting person that is worthy of being a main character.

What you don't want to do is make your character solely a martial arts expert—show him meditating and burning incense and living in a Shaolin temple.

Oh heck, even if he lives in a temple, make it a storefront in a city that is rented from a music store.

Then have him pick up the drums and join the heroine's rock band. Because of his fast hands, he is able to drum a special beat. Now you've added to the initial stereotype and created a possibility for uniqueness.

In my book *Jade: Perfect Match*, Aiden Lin is a martial arts expert—as a Navy SEAL—but he is also an aspiring writer.

Good in Math

Many Asians are good in math. Many are not. This is another stereotype that has nothing wrong with it. We need people who are good in math.

What else is your character good in?

If you add computers, then you haven't changed the stereotype much. If you make him nerdy and shy, you are still latching on to the math nerd stereotype. You have not gained many points.

Instead, add something unexpected.

Let's say your hero is good in math, and he's also a loudmouth Bible preacher. Do most people think loudmouth Bible preachers are good in math?

Let's add another dimension. Let's say your hero is the campaign manager for a young congresswoman.

You've now taken a stereotype and expanded on it until you have the possibilities for a unique character to develop.

Eats Weird Food

Well, some of this is true—but ...

Yet again, you don't want this to be the sole distinguishing characteristic of your hero or heroine. You should also allow for individual differences. Let's say your heroine loves durian [an extremely stinky fruit] and your hero hates it. Can't stand it. But he likes to tease her with balut [partially grown duck embryo boiled in the shell].

This can be an ongoing joke and a very interesting food fight; however, there's more to your hero or heroine than their food choices.

One food item is considered offensive, and that is the joke of eating dogs. Dogs are preferred pets in the Western world, so it is an emotionally fraught topic. The dog-eating trope was used by racists as a description of the Yellow Peril and why Asians should be excluded. Not all Asians eat dogs and cats or even bats and pangolins, and this particular dog-eating trope should not be touched, especially for Asians in Western countries.

The only reason to write about dog, cat, civet, bat and other strange animals as food is if you are doing a story with wet markets in Asia. In that case, set the story with multiple characters from different points of view and go into it deeper with more research and background.

While you can have fun with food, I encourage you to do more with food to avoid stereotyping. Explore cooking of various types, and remember, Asia is a huge continent ranging from the Near East to the Far East. Not all Asians use woks—most don't—and Asian fusion food, like Korean hot dogs, comes with all sorts of creative coatings.

Everyone loves food, so go for it and expand on the deliciousness—but beware of only concentrating on the strange and weird choices.

Asian people eat pizza too.

Robotic, Emotionless, No Fun

Another stereotype of Asians is that they lack emotion or are too studious to be fun. This is seen by popular depictions of staying inside to study or practice violin while other non-Asian characters are out playing sandlot baseball.

The Asian character is usually the follower or someone smart who provides data to the hero. In general, seen as lacking leadership skills or personality—the opposite of the life of the party, or robotic.

This is a harmful stereotype that was used by Harvard University to down score Asian applicants. During the lawsuit against Harvard, it came out that they used a point system in several categories. The lawsuit discovered that Harvard consistently rated Asian American applicants lower in the personality category. They were seen as not likable, lacking in courage, passion, kindness, with low leadership potential. This is in contrast to the interviewer's notes where a person who actually interviewed the candidate would point out the applicant as a passionate leader, enthusiastic and engaging, but the admission officer would lower the score.

I don't believe any of you would create main characters that are robotic, emotionless, and lacking in fun, but if you do, make sure it's a growth area for them. There's nothing wrong with a workaholic who learns to slow down once in a while. Some characters are more stoic and subdued than others, but as long as you expand on the stereotype and add other interesting traits, you are okay. Just be aware that this is a stereotype used to keep Asians below the glass ceiling.

Bad Driver

Okay, this one is plain mean. I mean it.

First of all, bad driver means different things to different people. It might be the guy doing thirty in the left lane on a highway or the aggressive driver cutting across five lanes to make an exit. In any case, this is one of those stereotypes that are untrue. I won't look up the statistics, but I'm betting accident rates are not significantly higher for Asian drivers than others.

I'd say use this one with caution if your story is a romantic comedy and you're making fun of someone's mother or a villain. But even then, it might be better to leave this one out, or do a contrasting one with a mother-in-law who is a reckless driver as opposed to timid.

Or make your Asian hero a NASCAR driver.

My hero, Teo, in *Roaring Hot*, is a motorcycle racer.

Viewed as Foreign or Different

This stereotype is viewed differently by different generations of Asians.

My parents who immigrated directly are happy to be seen as foreign. They don't particularly care if they fit in to American culture or not. They speak with an accent, and that's that.

Their children, us, were more embarrassed about their "foreignness" than they were. Sometimes, growing up, I envied them, because they at least accepted themselves. They knew who they were and why they came to a different country.

Second-generation Asian Americans are those who have at least one first-generation parent. They were born in the United States and usually consider themselves American.

However, because of facial features and having parents who are immigrants, second-generation Asian Americans have the most conflict with "fitting in."

The parents may require them to speak the foreign language at home and make them go to extra Saturday school and temple. Or the parents may forbid speaking the foreign language at home and make their children extra American by joining country clubs and Christian churches.

Either way, a second-generation Asian American feels the most "hyphenated" because he or she is straddling two worlds.

The second-generation person may react in three ways. Either embracing the home country completely and acting as if he is also an immigrant, although he feels peeved when a member of the home country says he speaks the language with an American accent.

He could also reject the home country identity completely and become more American than an American. He will likely overdo it as overcompensation and take on the attitudes and mannerisms of the dominant American community near him—whether white, black, or Hispanic.

This is why you sometimes see Chinese *cholos* or Asian hip-hop rappers. The person wants so much to belong that he or she becomes a culture chameleon.

The third alternative, of course, is the well-balanced one. The person accepts his hyphenated condition and is comfortable going between both worlds.

After the third generation, a lot of Asian Americans have either intermarried or are biracial or are embedded into their local communities. They may have a passing interest in their ancestral country, but they do not feel as conflicted as the second generation.

Some third-generations rebound toward the home country, especially if their second-generation parent was ultra-assimilated. By fourth or fifth generation, acceptance and appreciation of their heritage is usually attained, and the individual no longer cares if you ask "where do you come from?"

Therefore, when working up your Asian character, one of the most important characteristics is to discover which "generation" he is and how that impacts his identity.

The simple question, "Where are you from?" can be viewed differently depending on how the individual feels.

For most white people, it's a conversation starter. It's a way of finding out if you have something in common—for example, cheering for the same sports team or sharing experiences of Nor'easters. However, many Asians feel insulted because to their ears, the question, "Where are you from?" means "You don't look like you belong here. I'm asking you to remind you you're not from here so I can tell you to go back to where you came from."

A better conversation starter could be, "If you could live anywhere in the world, where would it be?"

Model Minority

This is another insidious stereotype of which nothing good will come of it. The Model Minority pits Asian Americans against other ethnic minority groups and serves to divide us from each other.

It is also untrue.

As with any community, some people achieve success and others do not. Some are financially well off and others struggle. A harmful stereotype like the model minority glosses over the struggles of disadvantaged people by basically saying, "If she can do it, why can't you?"

No one likes to be compared to a mythical standard, and therefore this stereotype is best avoided and utterly useless in character development.

It can, however, be used by the villain in trying to divide the hero or heroine from each other or another member of the community. However, thoroughly understand why the model minority stereotype is racist not just toward Asians but also toward other minority groups.

It gives Asians the appearance of success by working within the system while maintaining the superiority of the dominant culture. It holds Asians in the position of "teacher's pet" without questioning why there is a teacher in the first place.

Finally, by declaring Asians as "almost there," it allows Asians to internalize their second-place status and look down on those who are excluded. It keeps the power structure intact and entices Asians to aid and abet from a subservient position—thus perpetuating the stereotypes while dividing and conquering the unity of those who fight against racism.

Family-Oriented and Clannish

On the surface, being family-oriented and clannish are not stereotypes reserved for Asians. Many people are family-oriented, and no one is more clannish than the Hatfields and McCoys.

However, the stereotype when it pertains to Asians has a negative aspect when it comes to romance. [Note: I'm assuming contemporary romance rather than historical where the characters are bound to their culture milieu.]

The implication of family-oriented is that the Asian is not as interested in romantic love when choosing a marriage companion as a Westerner, for example.

This goes into the issue of arranged marriage, as a person would accept a mate chosen for him by his parents. He cares more about his parents' happiness than his own—or he doesn't much view romantic love as important, but that the wife will be a good mother, cook, and life partner.

Another part of this stereotype is that the Asian hero or heroine caters more to the group than herself as an individual. If the group or clan disapproves of her actions, she will adhere to their wishes.

This is a tough one. Of course, there are individual Asians who are more family-oriented and do see marriage as a business contract; however, not all feel this way. While there is respect for elders and the opinions of relatives, only a weak character would allow the clan to overrule her own agenda.

This stereotype can be defeated by making sure your character has clear goals and motivations as well as the individuality to strike out on his own when challenged by family.

Hero material would demand it.

Being family-oriented can also be a positive trait, because it means a man is looking for marriage. In many contemporary romances, especially those written for the mainstream, a stereotyped alpha male is usually a commitmentphobe. The strong, silent type who is a loner is a popular type of hero.

How welcome would it be to have a hero who actually likes women and wants to be in a committed relationship?

However, when writing a romance, you need conflict, so you might pair a family-oriented hero with a commitmentphobe heroine.

In any case, it's not negative to be family-oriented. Just be careful not to portray it in a way that makes for weak characters.

Submissive (Female)

This stereotype is more wishful thinking from the dominant white male culture than reality. While women in general were more submissive before the 1970s, contemporary Asian women aren't any more submissive than Western women.

Again, as with all stereotypes, they do not pertain to the entire spectrum of behaviors. Some individuals are submissive whereas others are aggressive. Sisters within the same family can exhibit opposite behaviors when it comes to obedience, submission versus rebellion, and confidence.

Therefore, this stereotype is next to useless when portraying a romantic heroine. The last thing you want in a heroine—a person with strong agency who makes her own decisions and pursues a worthwhile goal while being a capable match with a strong hero—is someone who can't think for themselves and allows everyone to run her over.

Your heroine could struggle with being a doormat, and her character arc would have her prevailing at the end of the story, but submissiveness is not solely reserved for Asian females, and hence this trait is irrelevant.

I would advise against using it for an Asian female. If you want to write a heroine overcoming submissiveness, choose another one that doesn't suffer from such stereotypes.

As for the opposite stereotype, the dragon lady, I for one am not that bothered by it since who doesn't love a badass?

However, make sure she is a fully developed character and as always, even with badass characters, show a soft side to humanize them as you do with the alpha male.

Target of Jokes (Male)

The goofy, nerdy, out-of-touch Asian guy who is the butt of all jokes is another harmful stereotype that is better left untouched.

This comes from marginalization of the Asian male into a character whose only role is to show how normal, well-adjusted, and heroic the other male characters are.

Cringeworthy examples are Long Duck Dong of *Sixteen Candles*, Leslie Chow from the *Hangover* movies, and Bobby Lee from *Harold and Kumar*.

I'm sure you can dig up more.

Being the target of jokes does not make a great romantic hero. Neither does using a friend as the target of jokes—like Harold does to Bobby Lee—make him particularly attractive either.

This area is fairly tricky to tackle, especially since a lot of the jokes fall to stereotypes: geeky, nerdy, can't get a girl, speaks broken English, and letting whites make fun of him in return for being "accepted" by a peer group. If you haven't had a chance to do so, search for the clips of the characters mentioned above.

People who would never think of making black jokes, fat jokes, or even blonde jokes crack Asian jokes all the time. You can find examples even in 2020. Usually, the jokes are aimed at Asian males or Asian children and families. For example, Chris Rock made a joke about nerdy Asian math kids and pulled them onto the stage at a recent Oscars Award Ceremony.

Rock then makes a joke, "If anybody was upset about that, just tweet about it on your phones. Also made by these kids." - Chris Rock

Everyone in the audience laughed—including big name stars like Leonardo DiCaprio were laughing and cheering, and it was even put as a highlight on *People* magazine. Jokes about Asian kids and child slavery are not only funny but acceptable by people who would never think of making jokes against other marginalized groups.

As recently as 2019, famous comedian Dave Chapelle believes it's okay to make racist jokes about Asians and take jabs at transsexuals. He then does a horrid mocking impression by making a "Chinese face" complete with accents and buck teeth. When called out on it, he attempts to deflect by saying his wife is Asian. Um ... to me that's even less of an excuse than just admitting you made a mistake.

Not only did the audience laugh at his portrayal, but Chapelle goes on to win the 2020 Grammy awards for Best Comedy Album.

The reason I point this out is because everyone knows better than to make degrading jokes about certain groups, but Asian men and Asian people in general are still viewed as fair game.

Of course, debate rages over "it's only a joke." Well, that's fine *if* Asian men are portrayed across the board with positive images to balance out the negative ones. If we had heroic, athletic, leader roles, then these "jokes" would not be the single image that the audience is accustomed to.

The disrespect for Asian men goes beyond racist jokes. It also deflates their level of strength, power, and heroism in action films.

This is the "order of death" in action films where Asian men are briefly brought in, only to die first. One of the first to die in *Hunger Games* is an Asian male. And while *Agents of Shield* does a great job with Asian American female kick-ass actresses, the very few Asian male agents are cannon fodder and disappear as quickly as they appear. Among them are Agent Quan (1 episode), Agent Kim (2 episodes), and Trevor Khan (4 episodes). In *Agents of Shield* Season 5, let it be noted that Agent Kim is the first one to die when the ship is attacked. They introduced him and I was hopeful he'd last, and then two episodes later, he was dead. Even though these men were not the target of jokes, they were shown as expendable props.

Whether the producers were aware of it or not, a large population of Asians were watching and likewise disappointed. While it's true that other characters die, the lack of representation for Asian males in heroic roles means that the few who appear on the screen or in a novel take on more significance.

Remember, the only purpose for degrading the Asian male as a target of jokes or "first to die" is to make another character look better. It certainly doesn't make him an attractive romantic lead.

These lame stereotypes are best avoided, and in these days of anti-bullying, making fun of a character will not endear you to most romance readers. If you want comic relief, try to make the character heroic in his own mind and overdo his arrogance so that a putdown is funny but does not demean him. Or if you have many Asians characters in your story (or an Asian-majority story), you can have more variety in terms of skills and humor like they did in *Crazy, Rich Asians*.

Although, one does wonder how it would have been received if a white character portrayed the nerdy brother who so obviously had a crush on the heroine. How easily we all laughed at him before feeling shame at enjoying a scene at his expense.

The bottom line is that we should portray Asian characters as you would any other character. Win some, lose some, hold some, and fold some.

Tropes to Avoid

Because Asians have been marginalized from mainstream Western literature, most of the standing works with Asian characters were created by whites.

The works from the twentieth century and earlier are especially problematic, because the authors saw Asians as strange, exotic, inscrutable, and mysterious.

If you've ever watched *Breakfast at Tiffany's* with Mickey Rooney as Mr. Yunioshi, you'll know how cringeworthy and unacceptable it is to put on yellowface and make a mockery of the Asian character.

The following tropes are the worst of the worst.

White Savior

The white savior trope is one of the most damaging tropes in literature. It portrays the white character as the smartest, brightest, most heroic and courageous human being who comes down into a bleak and backward community to lift the poor benighted inhabitants up out of their eternal misery.

While at it, the white savior, if he's male, usually attracts the oppressed and submissive females while fighting off the bad chauvinistic males. He walks off with the love of the highest status female in the story, because he is so much more worthy of admiration, gratitude, and honor than any of the people he lifted out of their lowly mucky existence.

Don't do it.

Examples of white saviors pertaining to Asians are the book, *Shogun* by James Clavell and movies starring Tom Cruise in *The Last Samurai* and Brie Larson in *Basmati Blues*.

Incidentally, even though Amy Tan is an ethnic Chinese writer and has done a lot of research in her writing, her books appeal to mainstream America because of her use of the white savior trope. In *The Joy Luck Club*, white male partners are depicted as more desirable than Chinese ones. In her book, *The Valley of Amazement*, the only male character who treated the heroine with any kindness was Edward Ivory [note the name, I mean, how much more obvious can you get?]. All of the Chinese men in the story, including the man who purchased her virginity, her father, and her eventual husband, are duplicitous, brutal, sexual abusers, and horrible. There is none good, no, not one [other than the white half-savior Edward Ivory who died in the flu epidemic of 1918 and was unable to lift Violet from her misery]. Anyway, Ms. Tan can write whatever she wants, and she is definitely successful in with the mainstream. However, I was clued into the problems of her depictions of Chinese males by an Asian male writer who told me while Asian females like the books and movies, most Asian males, if they bothered to read or watch, do not appreciate the depictions and believe them to be damaging. Another division in the community.

Female white saviors also exist, and they usually "dress up" or make presentable a male member of the oppressed group by helping to educate him, civilize him, and teach him the ways to behave. Of course, they tame the raw sexual energy of the male they save and turn him into a hero who wouldn't have made it without her wisdom, love, and devotion.

It's better to show your hero and heroine as emotional equals who can provide support and comfort to each other. They grow together while falling in love and heal the emotional needs of the other. This is, after all, one of the strongest messages of a romance. The hero and the heroine need each other, not from the position of weakness, but as true equals who open their hearts and blend their lives together.

Orientalism

Orientalism comes from a fascination of the ancient or traditional cultures of Asia while assuming that modern residents of those countries are still stuck in the time of their ancient civilization.

The Japanese are still living in the time of the samurai, going around with their *shotos* and *daitos* and burning incense in front of a suit of samurai armor of their venerable ancestor. The Chinese are sitting in their long robes writing calligraphy with a brush and memorizing the analects of Confucius, and of course, the East Indians are practicing tantric sex and going through every delicious chapter of the *Kama Sutra*.

You can find Orientalism in popular films like *Dr. Strange*, where his character takes off to Nepal and conveniently lands in the mystical temple of a white guru, The Ancient One, who teaches him all of the mystic arts, as if the only thing going on in Nepal is mystical studies of ancient whatevers.

Orientalism makes a fetish out of cultural artifacts and traditions, and the perspective is from the Westerner's viewpoint: different, strange, otherness, enduring, and timeless. It completely ignores the lives of ordinary people in the modern world while elevating ancient texts, myths, and superstitions.

The range of Orientalism goes from ancient Egypt and Jerusalem through the Middle East and the steppes of Central Asia, looping in the subcontinent of the Taj

Mahal and Southeast Asia, over the Great Wall and Mt. Fuji all the way to the Hawaiian Islands.

The natives are seen as stuck in time and dressed in costumes of their traditional cultures. They are there, timeless, waiting for the white Westerner to be fascinated, to learn from the guru, and to be transformed while adding a dose of white saviorism and mating with the highest status female.

Even films set in contemporary times are not immune to Orientalism. In the 2008 movie, *Body of Lies,* Leonardo DiCaprio plays a CIA Agent who speaks fluent Arabic and explains a passage from the Koran to his questioner. He self-righteously accuses his Arab friend of misinterpreting the one book he believes in and judges him wanting in morals. Obviously, he charms an Iranian/Jordanian nurse into becoming his love interest.

There's also a dose of white saviorism, although with a twist when the DiCaprio character says to a native, "We're here to protect you," and the man says, "You can't even protect yourself."

In stories exhibiting Orientalism, the people other than the Western hero are backdrops and props. The women spend their days behind veils, playing the lute, pouring tea, and arranging flowers in Zen-like peace.

The men work out with swords and magical spells, worshiping their ancestors and speaking with inscrutable Chinese proverbs.

Orientalism forgets that Asian people of today are modern people like the rest of the world. We use computers. We wear jeans and sneakers. We watch videos and listen to podcasts, and we chat on social media. We are like any other people in the twenty-first century, and we aren't kneeling on a silk cushion and burning incense any more than a modern American woman is churning butter while wearing a prairie dress.

While it's okay to include elements of Asian culture in your story, make sure your character is completely formed. He might be a tai chi master but he's also a business owner who has to deal with the city council member who opposes his permit. She is an archaeologist or museum curator and volunteers her time at a homeless shelter where a resident shows her an object he found.

Make your characters richly defined, including aspects of their Asian culture as well as their agenda in the modern, contemporary world.

Problematic Physical Descriptions

This is an absolute hot button issue. If you don't take anything else away from this book, please pay attention to physical descriptions that are offensive.

People in the United States are so sensitive to perceived racism that many authors are afraid to describe a person based on their ethnicity. You get coy references to almond-shaped eyes, light-tan skin tone, or wool-like hair.

I was reading *The Host* by Stephenie Meyer, and I can picture the annoying Seeker being of Asian descent, but she never states it directly. Maybe because it is a futuristic story.

Here is Ms. Meyer's description:

"She was very small. If she had remained still, it would have taken me longer to notice her there beside the Healer. She didn't draw the eye, a darkness in the bright room. She wore black from chin to wrists—a conservative suit with a silk turtleneck underneath. Her hair was black, too. It grew to her chin and was pushed back behind her ears. Her skin was darker than the Healer's. Olive toned." [Meyer, Stephenie (2010-04-21). *The Host: A Novel*]

In many stories, we are often left with a guessing game. If the author leaves out racial and ethnic tags, the assumption is the character is white. But if the author puts it in, some may object and say it shouldn't make a difference. Well, that's the point. It shouldn't make a difference, but in order not to be invisible on the printed page, I believe the author should make it part of the description so that the reader gets the entire picture of the world the author is describing.

Unfortunately, some of the description can be problematic. In my opinion, it's okay to state upfront or have the character introduce herself to the reader and get that out of the way. Once the reader has a picture in his mind, the rest takes care of itself without the author having to resort to stereotypical or offensive hints.

For example, in *Jade: Perfect Match*, Jade spots Aiden at the airport and describes him.

One man stood by himself. A tall, broad-shouldered Asian man with his nose buried in a thick paperback. His hair was cropped short and his skin had a healthy bronze glow, but he was overdressed for a tropical vacation, wearing dress slacks, polished shoes, and a white button-down shirt. [*Jade: Perfect Match*, Rachelle Ayala, 2018]

In *Dog Days of Love*, the hero gets it out of the way when he spots the heroine in the park with her dogs.

The pretty, but businesslike black woman was Dr. Vanessa Ransom, Ph.D. in Psychology, and an acquaintance of his other brother, Grady, who ran Dogs for Vets, a charity matching veterans to therapy dogs. [Ayala, Rachelle. *Dog Days of Love*, 2017]

That said, some authors prefer to not mention ethnicity or race, and they use descriptive markers to clue the reader in that the character in question is not generically white. In that case, care must be taken with the caveat that one cannot predict the future and whether words that were okay in 2020 are no longer deemed acceptable.

Which brings me to the point that mistakes are made and no one can predict the future. As soon as you've written the words, they become a part of history, and we should not excoriate authors who used terminology that evolved to mean something different.

The following are physical descriptions as pertaining to Asians that people might find offensive [quasi-2020].

ALMOND-SHAPED EYES

Did you know in China, almond eyes are used to refer to a dog's eyes? Bet you didn't know that.

If you want to describe a character's eyes as narrow, you can use slender but not slanted.

It's a shame that some words have been used in a derogatory context which takes them out of the vocabulary. Unfortunately, that includes slanted. Narrow may denote emotion, so it's hard to say whether to use it or not, and slender is a neutral term that gets your meaning across.

Finally, there is no need to say "Asian eyes" after you've already introduced your character as having Asian descent. It is redundant and points to the "otherness" of your character.

Although yikes! Pointed jewels?

Especially one so enchanting. Carina had glossy, straight black hair framing an oval face with a dainty nose and eyes like pointed jewels. [Ayala, Rachelle. *Whole Latte Love*, 2014]

YELLOW SKIN

Even though Jesus loves all the little children. Red and yellow, black and white, the terms "red" and "yellow" are no longer used to describe skin color.

Both of these colors have been used in a pejorative manner by prejudiced people. For example, the United States went through a Yellow Peril phase where Chinese people were driven out of small towns and cities all over the West. Many towns became Chinese-free zones, and even big cities like Seattle, Tacoma, and Santa Ana removed every Chinese person within their borders. They burned their houses and if any people happened to be caught inside, too bad. One witness described the stench of burning human flesh was sickening and almost unendurable. Even large cities like Los Angeles and San Francisco tried to drive out all their Chinese residents, although they failed due to the fact that the Chinese driven out of smaller towns gathered in Chinatowns.

Yellow peril politics whipped the population into a hysteria of fear of the unknown invader. The results cascaded through the following century: the Chinese Exclusion Act, the internment of Japanese Americans, national quotas limiting immigration from certain countries. In the present day, the demonization of Asian countries, like Japan's domination of the auto industry and the rise of China's economy, is used to scare and frighten the average American.

Finally, other uses of the word yellow are not positive. Yellow journalism, yellow-bellied, yellow jack, and yellow fever—all negative connotations.

Meanwhile golden is a positive word and used to describe blond hair. What's interesting is that the direct Chinese translation of blond hair is "yellow hair," but there is no negativity there.

In Asia, yellow is a positive color. It is the color of the sun and the solar chakra. Yellow is an imperial color representing power, royalty, and prosperity. It is considered a lucky color to attract good fortune to your household, and New Year's red envelopes are decorated with yellow-gold letters.

Ending on a funny note. Yellow is a color that draws attention and is the color of rain slickers and taxi-cabs. My parents believed yellow was the safest color for cars, so during my entire childhood, we were the kids driven around in giant yellow station wagons. [You may use this in one of your Asian character's childhood memory.]

As to how to describe skin color? Maybe you don't need to. Or if you have to, try and stay away from coffee, paper bags, nuts, caramel, and chocolates. Keep it simple. Pale-beige, light-tan, bronzed, dark-brown. Anything more poetic like "sheen of the harvest moon" or "jeweled ochre of the desert cliffs" is drawing way too much attention to your own purple prose.

"Nice try, Mr. Dee." I polish another glass, even though it doesn't have water spots. "My sister and I don't look a thing alike. She's taller, darker, with big brown eyes, the perfect Filipina. I look Chinese and have freckles." Not to mention a customer said I was chubby, and my sister Evie gave me a lecture about cholesterol and glycemic index right before going back to Boston. [Ayala, Rachelle. *Claiming Carlos*, 2014]

Obviously, Choco shows some bias in her self-deprecation, but this is her opinion of herself, so she's forgiven. We can assume she's opposite of her sister's description, and part of her character arc is to accept her self-image.

FLAT-CHESTED, SHORT, SKINNY

These descriptions use the average Westerner's body as the default standard and then describe the Asian person as a contrast. Instead, try to describe the Asian character in his or her own right. If he looks great to the heroine, then have her drool over him. No need to tell everyone his height and whether he's shorter than the white guy standing next to him.

Holy moly. Could God be so unfair? His heartthrob looks haven't changed a bit. If anything, he's filled out, his shoulders wider and the angle of his chin more confident. The boyish face, so instrumental in rocking him into boy band heaven years ago, has become rugged, more angular, his jaw stronger and dark with a five o'clock shadow. And it's not even noon. What's new are the tattoos criss-crossing his muscular arms. I'm too far away to tell, but the metallic glint over his lower lip could be a piercing. [Ayala, Rachelle. *Taming Romeo*, 2014]

Fetishes and Eunuchs

One way to marginalize a group of people is to stereotype their sexuality or sexual attractiveness. Because the white man is traditionally dominant in Western culture, all other men's desirability is made in comparison to him as the gold standard.

The way sexual marginalization is applied to Asians is to dehumanize the two genders in opposite directions. The Asian female is turned into a submissive and exotic sex kitten while the Asian male is emasculated and portrayed as an asexual nerd who is not even attractive to Asian females.

This unfortunately feeds into racial self-hatred and causes some Asian females to outright proclaim they don't date Asian men.

I'll pick this up later, but first, let me attack the fetishization of Asian women.

Asian Female Fetish

An Asian woman's smaller average physical size allows Western men to feel big and powerful beside her. Because early contact with Asian females were in

Gold Rush brothels and later on in conjunction with Western military power in occupied countries, the stereotype of an Asian woman is that of a sex worker, or at best, a war bride or seductress—eager to please the Westerner and to be rescued from her pitiable countrymen.

One of my most hated songs is David Bowie's "China Girl." I won't reproduce any of the lyrics here, but you can easily find it on the internet. Let's just say he has swastikas in his eyes; he thinks Chinese don't have televisions, and he believes we should be grateful for men who want to rule the world. This song personally hurt me because I was bullied by guys who ran around chanting the song to me and doing the *ding-ding-ding* tune. This is why we should note that even if you are enjoying a stereotype against someone else, you could be hurting a vulnerable young person and affecting others negatively by making them think the stereotype is socially acceptable. [As a side note, even if David Bowie is not prejudiced against black people, he can still harbor unhealthy biases with respect to Asians because of the pervasiveness of the stereotypes he believes to be true.]

The fetish by Western men for Asian women is all about domination and cultural superiority with a huge dose of white savioritis.

Later on, I'll talk about interracial romance and how you can still have a successful romance between an Asian woman and a white man, but now that you are aware of this thing called "Asian fetish," please remember that your character should never say things like, "I love dating Asian women," or "I have the hots for Asian women," especially as a pickup line. I once had a white guy say, "My girlfriend just moved out and she was Asian."

What a loser!

And once, when I was applying for a job, the white CEO of the company made a big startling motion when he met me, eyes popping, jaw gaping, and said, "You look just like my ex-wife."

Puh-lease. Asian women are not interchangeable sex toys who are ready and willing to step in when you need to change the batteries.

And we don't look the same.

Asian Male Myths

While Asian females are overly sexualized, the Asian male is stereotyped to be nerdy, geeky, and asexual. We've already covered the butt of a jokes stereotype, but this one goes even deeper and is more harmful to not just the psyche of the Asian male but breaks up the Asian community and pits the males against the females.

Worst of all, Western media has created a rumor that Asian men are small where it matters. Every man is concerned about his penis size just like most women care about their breast size. Whereas for women, bigger is not always better, men believe bigger is always better.

There are no scientific proofs that Asian males have smaller packages than other males, but the fact that people talk about it and some people attempt to measure and study this does enough damage.

Online dating sites have surveys that show 90 percent of non-Asian females won't date Asian men, and 40 percent of Asian females refuse to date Asian men—this is before even meeting one in person.

People who won't dream of saying something racist like, "I would never hire a white woman," believe it is okay to say they'd never date someone based solely on their race. It is especially hurtful for an Asian male to have sisters tell him she would never date an Asian male as she goes on dates with non-Asian men.

This kind of sexual differential destroys the Asian American community because of the effect of internalized racism. The Asian female who is fetishized has "dating privilege" compared to the male who is shunned. His response is to either hate himself or resent the privileged Asian female and exclude some other innocent Asian female from his dating pool.

As a side note, I have dated men of every race, and I have barked up the wrong tree of an Asian male who won't date Asian females.

Since Asian men are individuals with different personalities, different achievement levels, different outlooks in life, different facial features, different physical characteristics, there is no justification to saying you would never "date" someone based on their race.

The blame for this differential can be attributed to Western society's messaging through movies, books, and popular culture. Certainly, women in Asia do date and marry Asian men—no problem there.

However in Western cultures, Asian men have been denigrated as unattractive and undesirable—even to the point that when one of the hottest Asian men, the martial arts actor Jet Li, plays Romeo to a Juliet played by the African American singer Aaliyah, their kissing scene was deleted because focus groups showed that the general public [I'm guessing Western] is uncomfortable seeing an Asian man kiss a Black woman.

Incredible, isn't it? Romeo cannot kiss Juliet!

I've encountered my own Asian male rejection from a boxed set I wanted to join. I wrote a proposal to the organizer, an Asian author who has a following. She loved my story idea, but did not like that my hero was ethnically Korean.

Here is her note to me.

"Totally love the plot. My only reservation is the fact that he's Korean American. I did Japanese American before and except for American readers who are *otaku* themselves, the readers really didn't find my hero that hot. However, for another NA book, I tried another tack: my hero is European/Western in looks but adopted by Korean parents and even has a Korean name to boot. I would recommend (but of course Rachelle has the last say since this is her story) that she does something similar. I'm not saying I'm certain her book won't sell—naturally I can't predict that—but based on my experience, some readers might not be able to relate to it. =D [squinty-eye laugh out loud emoticon]

"I do understand the need to write characters we can relate to, but one thing I've learned is that you can still create characters that are Asian (in terms of personalities or even lifestyles) in every way but looks. :) [smiley emoticon] But again, that's just MHO. I'd really love to see Rachelle have more readers outside PH (I think I bought Taming Romeo but haven't read it yet) so that's why I'm hoping she can - even if it's just for this particular book - aim to be more "mainstream" with her characters." [email from organizer]

I have nothing more to say. If an Asian female romance writer of renown needs to create a character that is Western in looks [i.e. white] but Asian in culture, do we just give up the fight?

Absolutely not!

If you're reading this far into my book, I believe you are motivated to right this wrong. So please, join me in writing hot, hunky Asian male heroes who have all the qualities for a great romance and go forth to change hearts and minds at least in the bedroom!

By the way, I did exactly the opposite of what she recommended. My character, Jaden Sloup, has a Western name but an Asian face. He is of Korean descent but adopted by a white family. Here is an excerpt from *Played by Love*:

He [Jaden] crossed the street in front of the I-house. Ella was standing on the steps playing with her phone, oblivious to the admiring glances cast her direction.

For being a ditzy nerd, she was sure sexy. Thin, petite, but well-endowed where it mattered: full breasts, a cute perky ass, and a pixie spray of spiky blond hair framing her sweet heart-shaped face.

She was wearing black leather shorts with transparent tights and high-top black sneakers. Her black and white striped tank barely covered her midriff, and her fingernails alternated black and white. Silver and black wrap bracelets encircled her wrists and a gangster styled studded knit hat was propped over her head. There was no telling what she thought she was, especially with the spiked dog collar around her neck.

Instead of calling out, Jaden texted her a selfie with the corner of Bancroft and Piedmont behind him.

Her face lit with the text message and she opened it with a big smile. Giggling, she pointed her front camera at herself and snapped a selfie.

He snuck up behind her as she tapped out a message, and when his phone jingled, she swiped at her own phone. Her brow wrinkled when there was no incoming message.

"Boo." He was looking over her shoulder, inhaling her vanilla and cherry scented perfume, and wondering what she'd do if he snapped her collar.

Ella jumped and flung her hand back, hitting him in the jaw. Her late model smartphone went flying.

Jaden leaped off the stairs, diving with his arms outstretched. His ribs hit the curb and his knees scraped concrete. The phone skipped up, over his fingers, but as his chin slammed onto the asphalt he closed his hand around it, saving it from imminent and complete destruction.

Cheers and claps rang out from the international students gathered around.

"What a save!" a guy said.

"Wow, is he a goalie?" another voice said. "He didn't even try breaking his fall."

[Rachelle Ayala, *Played by Love*, 2014]

Developing Characters

Now that you are aware of the backdrop of Asian characters in Western literature and romance novels, it's time to develop your own unique and heroic character who happens to have Asian ancestry.

I trust that you regularly create characters who are well-defined, motivated, with talents as well as flaws, emotional strengths and weaknesses, and a familial backstory. They have friends, a business or career, live in their neighborhood, and exist within society like other characters.

The only additional detail is that these characters come from an Asian background.

Do your usual character development of picking a name, place, family structure, interests, hobbies, career, dating history, etc. As mentioned earlier, you can prepare the character's backstory by researching current and past history of his ethnic group, but it doesn't mean a lot of it gets into the story—unless a specific historical event is the main plotline.

If you're writing a romance, then you don't have to go into every aspect of Asian American history—only what is relevant to your particular story.

Let's make a list of additional questions you can ask your character as you interview him or her.

Country of origin, generation, family

- Describe your family tree. If any of your ancestors immigrated to the English-speaking country you are currently living in, how long ago and from where?
- Are you multiracial or multicultural? If so, please list and tell me something interesting about the mix of cultures in your family.
- Do your parents hold on to the traditions of the old country or are they trying hard to assimilate? Are there disagreements within the family on this?
- Did your parents teach you to speak a different language? If so, how well do you converse in it? Or did they require you to speak only English?

- What is your family's view of intermarriage? Which groups are acceptable or unacceptable?
- How do you deal with your family's view of your group of friends? Of people you're dating?
- Are your grandparents actively involved in your personal life? How do your parents treat them? How close-knit is your family?
- Do you or your family have an interesting immigration story? What did they learn from it and how did it color their thoughts about the new country they came to?
- If your family has been here more generations than most, what is their view of more recent immigrants? Do they identify with them or with the dominant culture?
- Are your parents more conservative or less conservative than you and your siblings? Are their values closer to the home country? List any values and outlooks you disagree with.
- Do your parents butt into your life or are they live and let live types? Do you wish they would stop interfering or wish they were more involved?
- How well does your family life fit into the Asian stereotypes? Are your parents strict? Do they ask you to eat all the time?

- What is your birth order within the family? Does it make you more or less responsible? Are you expected to help your parents take care of your siblings? If so, how do you feel about it?

Personal Asian Experience

- Do you resent others for assuming you are "foreign?" How do you react when someone as a conversational starter asks you where you're from?
- Recall a time when you were teased or made to feel different for being Asian. What happened and how did it make you feel?
- What is your opinion on interracial dating? Have you dated or married someone of a different race or culture?
- What is the most annoying stereotype you can think of for your ethnic group? Do you actively counter it or do you laugh it off?
- Would you end a friendship over a stereotype or a remark that shows bias?
- How much do you define yourself as either Asian or part of the dominant culture?
- Have you wished to be another race or ethnic group? If so, which group and why?
- Do you practice one of the traditional Asian religions or has your family converted to another religion? If you're converted, how

well do you feel accepted by the members of your new religion?

- What is the composition of the neighborhood you live in? Do the people "see race" or do they have a "everyone is the same" mentality? Does that bother you? Would you like to have some differences or would you rather brush them under the table?

- What kinds of foods do you cook? Do you prefer the food of your home country or are you pretty much of a mixed bag?

- If you could live anywhere in the world, where would it be? Would you be in the majority or minority?

- Do you believe a writer who is not in the same ethnic group as you can write your character and fully understand you enough to give you the partner of your dreams and a happily ever after? What advice would you give her?

- Is there any red flag you want the writer to be aware of, as in don't ever do this?

You can make up more questions and if you'd like to add a random question component, please see my book *366 Ways To Know Your Character* for a question a day to keep writer's block away.

Biracial or Multiethnic Characters

Out-marriage among Asian Americans is especially high these days, and you can easily find statistics that show the trend. Our society as a whole is accepting of interracial marriages, and our nation has many combinations of multiracial children who were born in the later part of the twentieth century who are now adults—ready for romance.

Many of them grew up in a mixed-race world of fully integrated neighborhoods. They are no longer the only biracial person they know, unlike several generations before them when people used to discourage intermarriage with the excuse, "but what about the children?"

This is all good news, of course, but it also means that the romances between your mixed-race characters will no longer have as its sole conflict the cliché where the parents disapprove of the dating partner's race.

I personally have not written any character who is "conflicted" about their background. While this self-doubt and angst was common fodder in a previous generation, most of the young people I meet, including my own children, are happy that they are multiracial and multicultural.

They feel a part of both backgrounds, as well as assimilating into the cultures of their friend groups, which also consist of many ethnic groups.

The other difference is the creation of a pan-Asian group identity that transcends the country of origin. While their great-grandparents could have fought wars on opposing sides and there was prejudice in the older generation based on country of origin, the Asians in America came to share a common experience—even if it started as people assuming they were sisters or asking, "Are you Chinese, Japanese, or Korean?"

When my mother arrived in America from China very soon after World War II, the first person she shared a room with at the processing station was with a Japanese immigrant. Six years earlier, the two countries were at war. Six years later, the immigration officials put my mother and the Japanese woman together, thinking they could communicate with each other.

My mother had a pleasant time, although communicating in broken English was hard. The same thing happened when she arrived in Texas, and they sent a Korean woman to show her around. She was then asked to visit a Native American man who was dying without any relatives. The Native American man held her hand and smiled, seeing a face that might at least pass for someone he knew long ago.

These days, mixed marriages within the Asian community, as well as between second- and third-generation Asian Americans and recent immigrants are common. Perhaps it's the result of the government glomming everyone together, or commonalities in culture such as respect for elders and a more conservative outlook regarding work and sex, but recent census data shows a reversal of the trend of Asian-white marriages back to Asian-Asian, although crossing country of origin backgrounds.

Vietnamese and East Indian, Taiwanese and Filipino, *sansei* Japanese and immigrant Chinese.

Think of all the possible characters you can create that can make your stories and romances that much more interesting. Think of the potlucks and parties, the weddings and baby showers as new families are forged, and my mother's saying, "From all four seas form families," comes true.

Interracial and Multicultural Romances

In the past, romance novels were segregated by traditional publishers and marketed to segments of readers. For example, Harlequin had a Kimani line that featured only African American romances. They were shelved in separate locations from the "mainstream" romances, and the assumption was that only African American readers would be interested in them.

With the advent of massive romance self-publishing, traditional publishers no longer dictate the classification of a romance or the categories they fit into. This has resulted in an explosion of romances that are marketed to all readers on the internet and social media.

Instead of targeting readers based on demographics, most self-published authors placed their books in the two categories they decided on and then marketed to whichever friends and followers they had. They ran giveaways and promotions with fellow authors, irrespective of demographics.

People met on Twitter or on Facebook, started chatting and exchanged books. Bloggers requested books from authors they met at virtual parties, and everyone downloaded freebies as long as the cover looked great.

Because the reader was no longer marketed to by large corporations, they were exposed to a diversity of books they would not have otherwise come across. Back in 2012, I joined several author groups, made both reader and writer friends, all on the basis of my historical romance, *Michal's Window*, which didn't fit the genres of my friends in contemporary romance, romantic suspense, historical fiction, memoirs, and whoever crossed my trail.

I formed a writing group that was diverse, gathering authors I met along the way, whether from my formatting business or online discussions. Most times, I didn't know why they joined my group, but I welcomed them all. We learned from each other, we cross-promoted, formed boxed sets, and in the process blurred the lines between different romantic subgenres.

We soon found out that readers liked reading characters of all cultures and ethnic groups. I also discovered a group of black romance writers who write Asian male heroes. There's even a subgenre designation called AMBW or BWAM stories for the Asian man, Black woman combination.

Strangely enough, Asian female and white male combinations are not marketed in a special way. Maybe these books simply blend into the landscape and are usually part of a series with other couples. In any case, some authors realized that having a "minority" character in their story allowed them to check a new category box and expand their reach.

Adding a Latino firefighter as a main character or a Latina interior designer gives the romance an additional category: Multicultural. African American romance has its own category, so having an African American hero or heroine adds two categories, Multicultural and African American romance.

This explains the recent expansion of multicultural romances and the demand from authors as well as readers to read romances with diverse characters. Furthermore, books with nonwhite main characters are making their way into mainstream romance—as they should.

Also, societal changes cannot be ignored, and many readers prefer reading literature and stories that reflect the world they live in.

In the past, a common theme or plotline for an interracial romance dealt with disapproving parents, friends, or community. Or the focus was on breaking racial barriers and dealing with cultural differences.

I personally don't write interracial and multicultural romances with the us-against-the-world tropes. You may, if you want, and obviously disapproving parents and relatives make for some deep conflicts. However, I believe this trope—forbidden love—is overused in interracial and multicultural romances and serves only to perpetuate stereotypes and normalize opposition to a relationship solely based on race and culture.

It's the tired 1950s cliché, "but what about the children?"

You're free, of course, to write about any subject and theme, but do realize that this ground has been thoroughly plowed over. Yes, opposition solely based on race exists, and racism is a huge problem—but you're hitting hot button topics and you must be prepared to do a lot of research and take the blowback if you show racism in your romance and don't exactly resolve it the way your reader believes you should. Add to that is the question of whether your couple truly "won over" whoever it was that was objecting.

If it was an ex-girlfriend and an expendable character, then throw a few cheap shots and get rid of her. However, if the racists are the parents on one side, then it is truly difficult to get that happy ending and convince your reader that the problems weren't just papered over.

I did a "Romeo and Juliet" type story with intransigent parents who hated each other because they were in opposing motorcycle gangs in *Bad Boys for Hire: Ryker*. How I ended it was quite final, but again, that is not the message to give when dealing with prejudice and racism.

Others have written interracial romances centered around a historical or current event—such as protest movements and uprisings. Usually, one of the characters is clueless or unaware and during the course of the romance, puts himself or herself in the shoes of the other character's struggles.

This is a very relevant theme and when done carefully, can help with the healing our society needs. My advice to you here is to interview many people and get their perspectives. Be sensitive to the ideals of movement and the real, gritty needs for the struggle.

Beware of your "unaware" character turning into an activist-tourist, in the sense that he or she is only visiting or playing in the sandbox, but that he or she fundamentally gets it by the end of the story. Beware also of any "savorism" from either partner. When done carefully, this type of story can be very powerful and a testament that love can build a bridge and heal a community.

As discussed before, making sure your hero and heroine are equals in agency is important, especially if one of them is white. I would avoid all of the privilege being on the white side, for example, making the white character the billionaire and the nonwhite character a maid or social worker. While it is realistic to contrast the natural environment of a white character versus a nonwhite character in society, since you are writing a romance and not a social treatise, my advice is to not make it a centerpiece of the romance, but one of the issues the couple has to deal with. Maybe your nonwhite character is ashamed that she stayed quiet while observing a white character exerting his or her privilege.

That happened to me when I was out with a group of friends at a Japanese hibachi dinner where we sat around a center grill where the cook chopped and grilled meat. A family with a Black man and his two teenage children, a boy and a girl, sat on the opposite side of me, but next to some of my white friends. We all waved and introduced ourselves, and one of my friends, in the effort to be friendly, praised the Black father for how he was taking his children out on a night on the town. She then asked about the teenage boy and girl what sports they participated in. She told them to stay in school and out of trouble. She thought she was being personable and nice. I was cringing on the opposite side of the cook who stood quietly chopping and grilling. I didn't know if I should say something, but I could feel the Black family's night being ruined. I wanted to drop into a hole but my friends were all smiling and chatting—well, maybe one or two realized what was happening, but no one said anything. You can show a scene like this without preaching, and the reader will get it. It can be a learning moment for the white hero or heroine or it can be left unsaid. However, beware of only making the story an education for your white character. Romance goes both ways, and both characters learn and grow from being in the relationship.

It should be obvious by now, but not all interracial couples involve a white person. I know this is a vestige from previous times when the world of romance and popular culture was white centric. *Guess Who's Coming To Dinner*, etc. There are many combinations of multicultural romance, and you should take the time to explore them. I, myself, am married to a Boricua [or Puerto Rican descended] man, and there was no conflict at all among our families with race or culture. My entire extended family on both sides has members of every major race and ethnicity and so does our friendship group.

We need more stories that get into the heart of what it means to be black or Asian or Hispanic or mixed race in the society we live in, and a romance can show the hope and create an uplifting vision for the future.

This is truly the right time to write interracial and multicultural romances. You can be a part of breaking down barriers and showing readers a world where people are respected as individuals deserving of self-determination and finding the love of their life no matter where they started their lives.

Book Covers

The majority of stock photos showing romantic couples are still white male and white female. This has presented a problem for writers of interracial and multicultural romance, as well as writers of Asian romance.

The situation has gotten better lately, and there are cover designers specializing in People of Color book covers, but the pickings are still slim for some categories, such as Black Woman / Asian Man couples.

I frequently browse stock photo sites for romantic couples of all types and have bookmarked hundreds of them. Whenever I see an Asian/Asian couple that works, I download the photo and make a book cover, even if the book is TBD [for example, *Getting Genie*]

I have also used couples where one of the models has a slight "Asian" look and is wearing sunglasses. I then invent a biracial character who could fit the book cover.

Because of the dearth of Asian male and Black female covers, I've observed clever use of Photoshopping to put two models together, either side by side, or back to back. The other way to get around this problem is to only show one person on the cover.

I do this in my *Bad Boys for Hire* series which show only the hero on the cover. This technique allows me to use different heroines without worrying about whether I can find a stock photo to represent them.

Other interracial romance authors have told me that they, too, have to sometimes resort to only showing the white hero on the cover. Some believe it makes their book sell better—not to have a minority female shown, whereas others acknowledge that it is an artifact of not being able to find an interracial photo to use.

The other option is to not use any people on the cover. I do this with most of the books in my *Christmas Creek Romance Series*, and that has allowed me to have two white male and black female couples—*A Christmas Creek Carol* and *Kitty, It's Cold Outside*, as well as an Asian male and white female couple in *A Christmas Creek Caper*.

I've included my book covers on the top of each chapter for your reference. I always feel like I won the lottery if I snag a hunky Asian man, and you'll see a book cover I made for a book I haven't written yet, *Bad Boys for Hire: Luke*, perched over the Appendix.

What Happens if I Get Criticized?

Dear Romance Writers,

Gather around and hear me out.

You are all storytellers, and you play an important role in our world. Your stories expand a reader's world and convey cultural values and messages. You pass the baton of fables and legends, adapting them for your audience, and paint vivid pictures of thematic importance.

Of good over evil.

Of love conquering all.

Of working together.

Of loyalty and courage.

You write romance because you are a believer of love, and your stories are happy and optimistic, full of hope for a better world.

You are inclusive, and this is why you are inspired to write a diverse cast of characters—to show that no one is beyond the limits of love and that everyone is worth loving.

You pour your hearts, souls, and tears into your story, and you mean well. You did your research; you found beta readers; you may even have hired sensitivity readers.

But alas, you go to check your reviews right before going to bed and a yucky one-star review rips your heart's work to shreds.

An author you don't even know decides to use your book for open heart surgery. Instead of emailing you directly and opening up a conversation, they go to social media and gather their followers against you.

What do you do?

* * *

First of all, take a step back and pour yourself a drink. I prefer warm turmeric almond milk, but anything will do.

Calm down and remind yourself that everyone has a right to their own opinion. While their opinion may not agree with yours, or they might have misunderstood you, they still have a right to speak out or express it.

After you finish your drink, read the criticism as dispassionately as you can. Maybe the points are valid. Or there is an alternative interpretation that wasn't what you meant.

Everyone makes mistakes. While writing this book, I went and found a description I made about "enchanting Asian eyes." I got out my formatting software and changed it and reuploaded the book.

You might not be self-published, in which case you can't easily change the book, but you can do what Nora Roberts famously did.

She put a lampshade over her entire catalog and simply stated that her own catalog may have sections that are "offensive, racist, [or] homophobic." She then apologized and said she would do better.

Of course, you're not Nora Roberts, and no one would dare attack the grand dame of romance, so maybe your apology doesn't have the same effect.

However, it does de-escalate the situation and shows you are open to learning.

If you believe they're wrong or misinterpreted your story, or you meant to write a white savior story because it's realistic in that historical time period, then you can choose not to engage. It might be hard to do, but these days, with the quick trigger social media feeding frenzy, engaging only causes a situation to blow up.

If it's a one-star review, leave it alone.

If it's a Twitter gang up, take no notice.

Let it go.

For example, earlier in this book, I criticized Amy Tan's *The Valley of Amazement* for her white savior character, Edward Ivory. Do you think she cares? Nope. She must have meant to write that character exactly the way she did. She has editors and early readers, and she knows what she's doing. She wants to sell books, and her publisher knows what tropes sell the best. She's making mint off the book, so her best strategy is to ignore the criticism. A few disgruntled Asian males are not her readership anyway, and so what if she hurts their lives by perpetuating stereotypes? It's their fault they were born into the Asian patriarchy, and in her mind, she is absolutely right to call it out. If they can't see that they're not responsible for anything done by fictional characters, then it's their problem.

You get the gist.

You cannot please everyone.

There will always be someone who doesn't like what you write and not just because you have an Asian character. You are creating art, and once you release it, it becomes part of the public discourse. Someone will always criticize your work. Your choice is how you deal with it. My recommendation is to ignore it. And if you can't, then I would recommend you write the books you love but don't publish them.

* * *

A note to readers or writers who object to someone else's characters or plots.

In order to be constructive, if you see or interpret something that you feel needs to be corrected, the first step is to contact the author privately and engage them in a dialogue. Maybe they didn't realize that something they wrote is offensive, or they had a different motivation in mind and the words came across in an unintended way.

They are actually curious and interested in how their words affect others, and they may learn something from you. Approaching an author in the spirit of collaboration can create conditions of trust and learning, so I highly recommend establishing a relationship before attempting to correct someone.

Realize also that people have blind spots, and that also includes you. People view the world through different filters, and their interpretations differ based on their experiences.

If the author doesn't agree with you or does not respond, then my advice is to leave them alone and write your own book where you portray your characters in a way that fits into your view of the world.

Of course, you can do what you want, but in these days of social media fights, you never know how something might rebound on to you in a way you didn't expect. Or someone else suffers collateral damage, and no one wins over anyone else.

At least that's my opinion.

Natural consequences, karma, or whatever happens, and you don't need to be in the middle of it. Realize you can't fix someone else and move on.

* * *

Finally, let me address the elephant in the room.

What if you are a white writer and you are called out on either perpetuating a stereotype, accused of cultural appropriation, or told to stay in your own lane?

You will make mistakes, and so will anyone else. That's a given, however you will also learn. If the perpetrator is unsatisfied after you've politely addressing the objections, you've done your part.

As hard as it is to take the lumps, my advice is for you to "stay the course." You decided to be an ally and write romances with Asian characters because you wanted to increase representation. You wanted to help stem the tide of the danger of having "few stories," which of course magnifies the impact of any one representation.

You actively took up the sword to subvert harmful stereotypes and tropes, and you did your homework.

If the objection is that you should stay in your own lane, then the problem is with the closemindedness of the objector.

You are not appropriating anyone's culture by writing about them. If done respectfully, which I'm sure that was the spirit, you are adding to the many stories and giving your voice to the overall world culture by telling this particular story.

Finally, one person's view of perpetuating a stereotype is another person's attempt at extending and enriching it. You cannot fight what's in the objector's mind. He or she was triggered by something from his or her own experience. It had nothing to do with your story, but the filters they brought to view it through.

Therefore, again, stay calm and stay the course.

Do not get defensive and strike back.

Take another drink and chill.

Then start your next book with two more great characters. You don't need anyone's permission to write the stories that your muse serves up. No one owns your imagination or polices your thoughts.

I wrote this book because I want other people to write about our communities. I want more representation, and I want allies to destroy harmful tropes and stereotypes by writing well-rounded and heroic Asian romantic characters—especially the Asian male hero, so that real conversation is engaged and the lives of real people are improved.

Collectively, we can start a movement where people are judged by what they do and the content of their character, and to do that, we need more stories.

Example Excerpts

Asian Female Dating Privilege

Jade is peeved that an Asian man would talk to her and decides at least his English is perfect. She is used to being approached by men and naturally assumes the man is interested in her. [From *Jade: Perfect Match*, Rachelle Ayala, 2018]

Jade's gaze lingered on him a moment too long, because he lowered the book and caught her staring. She quickly looked away, annoyed as he sauntered toward her.

It figured they were the only two Asian people at the baggage claim, and he would automatically assume they had something in common.

Jade's mother was Chinese, but she didn't speak any language other than English. She oftentimes felt out of place in her San Francisco neighborhood where strangers automatically greeted her in Chinese.

She resumed staring at the empty baggage carousel as if mesmerized by the revolving metal leaves.

"Guess everyone's on Caribbean time," the man said. His deep voice drew delicious chills over her skin, despite the warm humidity soaking through her clothes.

"Yep," she said, not making eye contact. At least his English was perfect, without an accent. Jade hurried to check her cell phone, then dashed a text message to Dani.

[text messages to friend]

The man thankfully walked off, letting Jade breathe easier. He had an unsettling effect on her, as if his presence demanded her full and complete attention.

Jade caught her breath and tried to calm her palpitating heart. The heat didn't seem to bother the natives and the other tourists, but it sapped her concentration and made her light-headed.

[more text messages to friend]

"Miss," the Asian man said. "I picked up your luggage."

"How do you know which ones belong to me?" Jade asked. Her eyes met his, and she gulped. He might not be six-feet-four, but he was hunky and hot. Square jaw, heartbreaker eyes, high cheekbones and lips that would have been pouty if they weren't smiling at her.

"No one else here would be called Jade." He lifted the tail end of his long eyebrow. "Where are you staying?"

"I'm not telling you. How do I know you're not some weird stalker?" Jade ignored the text message chime on her cell phone.

At that moment, a chauffeur approached, carrying two signs. "Ah, I see you two have met. I'm Georges, the concierge from Perfect Match. Welcome to Ile d'Amour, the island of love. Miss Reed, Mr. Lin, let me drive you to The Secret Heart Villa where you'll be spending the week together in luxury and privacy." [Rachelle Ayala, *Jade: Perfect Match*, 2018]

Asian Family Dynamics

From *Playing Fastball*, Timmy Li suspects Tina Lee of gold-digging his wealthy father, Yan Li (Baba).

A couple minutes later, laughter and footsteps reverberated from the showroom garage where his father kept his collection of sleek sports cars.

Timmy's lips curled up in a snarl when he recognized the young, squeaky female voice. It was

Tina, his Baba's "pet," taking advantage of his dad again.

"Where've you been?" Timmy slammed the beer glass on the counter and squared his shoulders toward the kitchen door.

Two dusty figures shuffled through, dragging dirt with their sneakers.

"I crushed them, didn't I?" Tina's face glowed as she slumped her backpack on the kitchen chair—the expensive leather-backed chair.

She was a no-good ex-con, a grifter who'd perfected the waif-like orphan look which made his father feel sorry for her. Her sandy-colored hair was flat and lifeless, and her face was covered with smudges. Tattoos raked the backs of her hands and traced up her arms, and she was a skinny, boyish creature in her ripped jeans and cowboy shirt. Well, almost boyish if he didn't count the set of nice breasts and roundish ass cheeks she hid underneath her grunge-styled rags.

"You sure did. Five in a row." Baba raised his hand and high-fived the wastrel.

"Five what in a row?" Timmy glared at his father. "I pitched a no-hitter today. Everyone's celebrating at The Hot Corner. I came home to find you, and you're missing. Why weren't you at the game?"

"It's only spring training," his father said. "Tina and I had a wild idea to go monster trucking. They had an opening—a last-minute cancellation, so we grabbed it."

"We had a great time, didn't we?" Tina fist-bumped Baba and opened the refrigerator as if she belonged there. "I'm starving. What do you have?"

"Nothing, unless Timmy cooked," Baba said. "Hey, let's get cleaned up and go to The Hot Corner for dinner. We can celebrate your no-hitter."

"I don't feel like celebrating." Timmy shot daggers at Tina, the interloper. "Not if she's coming."

Baba's eyes narrowed, and he poked Timmy in the chest, hard, the way he always did when he had something bad to say but couldn't say it because "outsiders" were around.

Timmy gritted his teeth and snarled, but he didn't dare poke his father back. He was, after all, a dutiful Chinese son. His father had supported his baseball career one hundred percent—sending him off to training camps, hiring the best coaches money could buy, and after his mother passed away, moved to the United States to live with Timmy so he wouldn't be lonely.

"I think I'll hit the showers," Tina said after downing a can of soda in one long swallow.

She hefted her heavy backpack and wandered from the long kitchen followed by Blondie, the dog Baba had gotten from Tina when she swindled people at the pet rescue she got fired from.

Timmy tried to see red as he watched her go, but his seriously disturbed body perked up at the alluring sway of her hips.

Dammit. All those meals Baba fed her was filling her out—dangerously.

Timmy dragged his gaze from Tina and turned toward his father. "How much are you paying her to play with you?"

Poke.

This time, it hurt.

His father grunted and left the kitchen, leaving Timmy to stew in his own mixed-up juices.

Tina was much too young for Baba, and she was using every trick in the book to become the next Mrs. Yan Li.

No way.

Not over, under, and around Timmy's very alive body.

[From *Playing Fastball*, Rachelle Ayala, 2018]

Asian Fantasy Firefighter

Johnny Wok is no ordinary martial arts master. He is a firefighter, the son of the Kitchen God, and he fights kitchen fires in a unique way in *Black Tied: Sapphire* by Rachelle Ayala. [Precious is Sapphire's pet cockatiel.]

Which is why I don't blink even an eyelash when a Chinese superhero type jumps out of the monster thirty-six-inch wok. He lands with his feet and legs in front of my nose and immediately, the area around me cools. Instead of a gas mask and flame-retardant suit, he's wearing a black tank top and kung fu pants. He immediately gets into fighting position and makes circles with his hands and arms.

Um, I'm in need of a firefighter here, one with axes and water hoses, not a guy doing tai-chi like the old people in the park.

But he seems to be pushing the fire with his hands, sparring and almost dancing with the flames. His motion is fluid like streams of water, while his muscles strain and bulge in the sheer effort of grappling with the raging inferno.

From my vantage point on the floor, I can't help but notice his nice, tight ass, and the way his thighs bulge. I watch transfixed as he pushes the flames into a tiny ball, before setting it on the brass offering plate. It stays still, like a tiny marble of orange and silver.

The strange man puts his hands together and prays, bowing to where the cartoon images of the old-fashioned Chinese man and woman had been.

"Who are you?" My mouth unhinges enough to croak.

I'm still holding Precious close to my chest when the man turns in my direction. He throws a whitish powder all around the kitchen, his movements powerful like he's doing a kung fu form, you know, the ones with moves like Dark Dragon Draws Water, Angry Leopard Charges Rock, Cloud Hands Gathering Pearls, or Wild Horse Kicks Crane.

I'm so mesmerized I forget I'm dead, or at least push that disturbing thought to the back of my mind.

I've never been one to drool at firemen, mainly because I'm too uptight and I don't have a thing for big bulky muscles.

But this guy, he's strong, yet compact, powerful without the bulk, and oh, so leopard-like in his moves.

I bring Precious to my face, but she's motionless. At least we're together. "Look at that man move. Is he the Black Guard sent from the Underworld to escort us to the judgment seat?"

The healing powder does the trick, and all the soot and smoke is gone, leaving the kitchen sparkling and spotless. The smoke alarm cuts off, and the air is fresh and odorless.

Now the man sees me, and he stands in front of me, offering me a hand. I take it, and he pulls me to my feet so fast I stumble into him, bumping against his yummy chest.

"Who are you?" My voice comes out husky, more like a come-on than a challenge.

"I'm Johnny Wok." He rights me, with two hands on my upper arms. The dark-brown orbs of his eyes are focused on me, and I squirm from his intense focus.

"I'm dead, aren't I?" I blabber, still caressing my little bird. My throat lumps up and tears sting my eyes. "My Precious is dead, too, and it's all my fault."

"Let me see your Precious." He stretches out a large, square hand. A scar rises from his wrist, webbed like the shape of wings, like a bird rising from a fire.

"She was standing there preening herself. I didn't realize the smoke would kill her. I shouldn't have kept

her with me. I shouldn't have become the apprentice."
I place the limp bird in his hand.

He blows on her.

Nothing happens.

He blows again while rubbing her between his palms.

"You'll crush her," I protest. "Can't you throw some of that magic healing powder on her?"

"You mean my cleaning salts?" Johnny frowns, handing Precious's limp body back to me. "Doesn't work on living creatures. I'm afraid I can only do first aid, not bring your bird back from the dead."

"Are you a fireman?"

"Nope. Son of the Kitchen God." He points to the altar overlooking the stove. The unfortunate picture of the couple dressed in Chinese garb is burnt beyond recognition. "Those are my parents."

"Your parents are gods?" I hold Precious out like a precious offering. "Can they save my bird?"

He waves at the remnants of burnt offerings in the brass plate. "Seriously? Orange peels? Cigarette butts and empty bottles of wine and whiskey. You're lucky I didn't let your kitchen burn down."

"It's not my kitchen." Truly a dumb thing to say when I'm either dead or in need of a paramedic for birds.

"My bad," he says, flashing me a crooked and way too sexy grin.

[From *Black Tied: Sapphire* by Rachelle Ayala, 2017]

Asian Meet-Not-So-Cute

Bad boy Teo is told by his grandmother (Oba-chan) to bring a Japanese girl to her birthday party in *Roaring Hot.*

"Not really," Teo said, his eyes narrowing. None of the overly made up women would be the least bit appealing as far as Oba-chan was concerned. She'd been sending him pictures every day—granddaughters of people she knew, every one of them innocent and sweet, looking like their idea of a Saturday evening was a Hello Kitty pajama party.

"What do you get when you cross a mattress and a wanna-be actress?" Ronaldo laughed and slapped his thigh at the anticipation of his own joke. A bad joke.

"I'm out of here." Teo grabbed his towel and stepped into his flip-flops.

"Wait, wait," Ronaldo said. "I'll ask my grandma. She's sure to know of some starving actress who'd play the part."

"Actress? You're kidding. I'll find my own date." Teo scoffed at the notion he'd need Ronaldo's grandmother's help, even if she was the legendary Amanda Silver, the talent spotter who'd casted Hollywood's most memorable roles. He doubted she would be able to find an Oba-chan approved girlfriend—unless she recruited from Asian housewife schools.

"Hear me out." Ronaldo rubbed his hands as he always did whenever he had one of his harebrained schemes. "We put in what we're looking for in my grandma's database and pull out their contact information. I tell them my dad's producing a documentary on motorcycle Grand Prix racing. Instant girlfriend until your grandma's birthday."

"I'm not paying anyone to be my girlfriend." Teo sidestepped around a group of young men licking tequila shots off a model's body.

The entire scheme was too harebrained. Teo was a professional motorcycle racer on the pro circuit. He had absolutely no intention of seeing a woman twice, much less date anyone exclusively. But Oba-chan had given him a challenge and a deadline. And what Oba-chan decreed, Oba-chan got.

This party was a waste of time. He'd do better stalking teachers at the Japanese language training school. Racing around the cabana, Teo headed toward his Suzuki Hayabusa motorcycle parked on the circular driveway.

Ahhh! A woman squealed, and her drink splashed as she stumbled and planted her face into his chest. Her straight black hair flung like a curtain in front of her.

"Sorry, miss." He grabbed both her arms to steady her. A jolt of electricity shot through him and had his hands tingling. Who was this creature? Her bikini-clad body was slender and trim, and her skin glowed like fine porcelain. She was definitely Asian, either Chinese or Japanese.

"My contact lenses." Her breath hissed between clenched teeth. "Ow, ow, they sting."

"Did you drop them?"

"No, I have to get them out. Were you wearing sunscreen?"

"Well, yeah, sorry." He guided her into the pool house. "There's a restroom in there."

"Thanks." Not looking up, she fumbled with her purse and stepped into one of the changing rooms. She wore no ring where it counted.

Teo's gaze didn't leave the changing room door. Was this a stroke of fate? An eligible woman, possibly Japanese, had landed almost in his lap. And even better, she was pretty. Cute, kissable rosebud lips, a pert nose, slender eyebrows and smooth, silky hair a mile long.

A minute later, she stuck her head out the changing room door, her eyes blinking. "Mister, could you find my friend Peter?"

"Sure, what do you need?" Teo noticed tears running down her cheeks. Her eyes seemed swollen, although she did her best to cover them.

"I need someone to remove my contact lenses. I washed and washed my hands, but the Tabasco sauce isn't coming off and my eyes sting."

"I can do it, hard or soft?"

"Soft lenses, but find Peter. He's tall, lanky, probably hanging out with the other PA's, I mean personal assistants. They're usually at the bar playing models and bottles."

She still hadn't looked him full in the face. Teo cupped his hands over her shoulders. "Your eyes are burning and it's my fault."

Of course, her distress brought out all the male protective reactions in him. Here was his chance to score points with a vulnerable female. He puffed his muscles, steered her into the changing room and shut the door.

"I don't like anyone poking their fingers in my eye except Peter," she whined. "He does all my makeup."

Teo's gut clenched, not liking this Peter already. "I wear contacts too; let me wash my hands."

She stood still while he washed his hands.

"Open your eyes," he coaxed her.

"I can't, they're burning. I stuck my finger in and made it worse."

"Let me get it for you." He feathered his fingers over her smooth skin and gently propped a lid open, but he couldn't get the swiping motion correct since he was only used to removing his own lenses. He also couldn't help noticing her fine narrow eyes, very Japanese—and very, very alluring.

She pushed his hand away. "Stop it. You poked my eye."

"I can get it, but only if I pretend it's my own. Let me try. Stay still." He was nowhere done with being a hero, especially if the damsel in distress was such a cutie.

Carefully, he stepped behind her and rested her face on the side of his, then wrapped his arms around her.

Yum. Her scent, a hint of coconut sunscreen with floral accents made him want to kiss her, but he'd better control himself and get that contact lens out. After earning her eternal gratitude, she would no doubt reward him.

He could do it. Easy. With his left hand, he opened her eye and rubbed the soft lens gently with the middle finger of his right hand.

"Where's your case?" He could feel her heart fluttering and her breath tighten in small, nervous pants.

"Just toss it. They're disposables. Thanks." She dabbed at her eye, blinking.

"Okay, the other one. It's hard to prop your eye open, let me know if it hurts."

The eyelid was so tight it kept slipping, and it was difficult to concentrate with the electricity arcing between them. She had to be feeling it too, the instant chemistry. Teo didn't believe in love at first sight, but lust at first contact? Definitely. One more lens before the kissing started. Patience.

He murmured reassuring sounds while enjoying the intimacy, trapping her cheek to cheek. After a few more tries, he was able to extract the second lens and toss it in the trash.

Time for the reward. Heat crashed over Teo and he prepared himself for her gratitude. He'd be controlled at first, but before she could take the second breath and pull away, he'd turn her into his arms and kiss her senseless.

"Thanks." Her voice was small as she dabbed her eyes. "You can leave now."

Leave? That was it? He'd helped her, and she didn't even care to ask his name?

[From *Roaring Hot* by Rachelle Ayala, 2014]

Who Am I?

What qualifies me to write a book about developing an Asian romantic character?

Hmmm ... Thinking, thinking ...

I've lived only one life and have my experiences growing up in the United States in my Chinese American family. I'm also a romance author who has [as of 2020] written and published over sixty-five complete romance novels and novellas, as well as several non-fiction books on romance writing.

My extended family is an academic family full of scientists, doctors, engineers, one astronaut, and one Broadway show starlet. My parents arrived in America in the 1950s as college and graduate students. After getting their degrees, my father got a job as an aerospace engineer and moved us to Southern California.

I grew up in a neighborhood that had only one other Chinese family and one or two Japanese families. Our community was a well-blended one with approximately a third white, a third Hispanic, and a third black with a large contingent of Filipinos and Samoans. I went to high school in the late 1970s in an integrated environment where everyone wanted to get along, and I consider myself blessed to be a Banning High School Pilot Class of 1977.

Because I did not live in a Chinese American community, I had limited knowledge of cultural traditions. I did not go to Chinese school, did not have any social events or celebrations to go with Chinese New Year. I did not belong to a peer group dominated by any particular ethnic group. My friends are always just friends and a collection of people I got along with irrespective of ethnicity or race. Other than occasional trips to the Los Angeles Chinatown where we went to eat, our family lived like the other families in my neighborhood. We went to the park on Fourth of July, hid eggs on Easter, and wore green on St. Patrick's Day. I did, however, bring fried rice to any potlucks we had.

In college, I lived in an International Students dormitory, but I did do a lot of reading on Asian American history as well as took general education courses on the US/Mexican border. Wherever I went and whoever I met, I always listened when people talked about their families and adventures, picking up tidbits of culture wherever I went. I also had roommates from everywhere, and we shared cooking tips as well as talked about boyfriends and family. I won't disclose the variety of men I dated, because some things are better left under the covers.

After a career in computer science, I retired in 2011 and devoted myself to writing fiction. I've always dabbled in writing and just recently discovered some notes I made for myself on a mystery I was sketching out in the late 1980s. However, I got busy writing software and raising a family, so my writing was mostly technical.

Unlike other writers I know who started with women's fiction or literary fiction, I only ever wanted to write romances. To me, love stories are the best stories, and whenever I watch a movie or read a news story, I'm always looking for the love plot.

In the spirit of writing what I know, after I finished my historical Biblical romantic fantasy, *Michal's Window*, I wrote *Broken Build*, a romantic suspense set in Silicon Valley where the main plot revolved around building software.

My heroine, Jen Jones, is a build engineer and she's everything I wanted to be. I'm vertically challenged, or short, and Jen is tall. I'm not athletic, whereas Jen is a fast runner. Jen was not Asian though. She was a mixture of Puerto Rican and Cajun, but her heritage did not play much in the story as much as her software prowess and ability to fight, take pain, and keep on spinning builds while being kidnapped, beaten, and falling in love with her boss. Jen's friend, Vera Custodio, became my first Asian American heroine in *Knowing Vera*.

I didn't think about writing an Asian hero until I'd gotten to know a group of Filipina romance writers. I joined an online group led by Mina Esguerra to write a novella in a short time period—less than a month. We wrote every day and shared on social media what we were writing—tidbits such as the cute meet, the first date, the first kiss, and how *guapo* our hero was. Mine was Romeo Garcia, an actor who plays a bad boy in a soap opera. After *Taming Romeo*, I worked on *Claiming Carlos* and had no clue that writing romances with Asian characters was controversial.

That innocence lasted until I tried to join a romance anthology headed by a different Asian author and a white romance author of some fame. They formed a publishing company and many of us from Mina's class submitted for the boxed set. They specified a Western setting, i.e. in America or Australia but they did not specify "white" characters. I guess it was assumed when they said Western setting.

While they might have had other problems with my submission, *Playing the Rookie*, and I appreciate the feedback they gave for my rejection, the following paragraph was hurtful, especially as it came from the Asian romance author [not Mina].

One of our major requirements for the bundle is for the story to have Western settings and characters because those are the things our target readers expect to read. IR romance is a great market to write to, but it's not our target market for now. Your hero and heroine are both Asians, and sadly, this could make it hard for some readers to relate to them for the simple fact that they don't know much about Asians or how our cultures work. [rejection email].

I took it in stride and self-published Jessica Song and Jay Pak Ahn's hot and steamy novella, *Playing the Rookie*. My critique partners were more upset over this than I was, but after that, I wondered why readers did not want to read about Asian heroes and heroines. I also wondered if I had made my hero white or my heroine half-white/half-Asian, if they would have been better accepted.

I then experimented with many combinations of heroes and heroines [see Appendix for list of books]. While my own readers snapped up anything I wrote and loved the diversity, when I put out a boxed set titled *Rich Asian Lovers*, I got feedback from both Amazon and others that they did not like me using "Asian" in the title. Amazon claimed I used a keyword in the title to game the system. I asked my writer friends to ask their readers for feedback on the title and the content of the boxed set, which I changed to the generic title, *Spicy After Dark*. Because my writer friends are not Asian, the feedback from their readers was honest. Some said they didn't think Asians were romantic, and others thought I was better off not mentioning Asian in the title because no one believes Asians can be lovers—ever.

What were they thinking, that Asians only had arranged marriages?

The final disaster happened in a boxed set I was invited to join. It was initially called *Kiss Me: An Asian Hero Boxed Set*. The Lead invited a number of romance writers she personally knew and liked to write a sweet romance featuring an Asian hero. The idea was to promote Asian heroes and diversity in romance writing.

The authors all had different backgrounds but were excited to show the romance world that Asian men can be great romantic heroes.

I didn't end up making the boxed set, because my story, *Playing Fastball*, about a Taiwanese baseball player and a white foster child grown up alienated from her foster sister, was too long and I didn't make the dates.

The boxed set went out and readers loved it, especially Asian readers who were thrilled to see an Asian hero. However, a few white romance authors and readers objected to the title and accused the boxed set authors of fetishizing Asian men. They took their complaints to Twitter and soon, the mob attacked the boxed set.

Never mind that the attackers didn't bother reading the stories in the set and how the heroes were portrayed with love and respect. All they cared about was the fact that female authors who appeared visibly "white" dared to write a boxed set with "exotic and fetish-provoking" Asian men. And even added 1-star reviews to the set, even though they hadn't read any of the stories.

The attack pointed more to the stereotyping done by the drive-by complainers than the actual content of the boxed set. They read the title and cover picture and decided the set was "problematic."

One attacker went to one of the author's blogs and asked why they did not have a single "token" Asian author on the set. Again, this attack points more to the mindset of the attacker who is projecting her own prejudices than on what actually went on in the set.

I responded that I was invited to the set but my story was too long and didn't make it. Everyone who actually read the set was happy with it and the Goodreads page is filled with good reviews. The only objection people had was that there wasn't a visibly Asian author in the set!

But should that matter?

Each author had had their story not just edited but checked with Asian readers to ensure their heroes were authentic. Some of the authors in the set were biracial or in a relationship with Asian men, but did they have to "wear" those "creds" on their sleeve?

Incidentally, the people having problems with the set were all white people. Go figure.

Which brings me to the problem we have today about complaining on the one hand that we don't have enough diverse books with diverse characters while on the other hand accusing people of cultural appropriation when they do step out of their comfort zone to write characters that differ from them in terms of background.

One romance author, not in the set, confessed privately to the Lead, that after watching the social media hate outpouring at the authors, that she would **never** write a hero that was not white.

How is this good? That authors who try to write diverse characters are attacked on social media and their books are also attacked with bad reviews.

If we want authors to write diverse characters, we need to trust that they have researched and done everything correctly. They are, after all, storytellers.

As a side note, Lisa See, who I greatly admire, writes historical novels set in China and America with Chinese, Chinese American, and Japanese American characters. Her latest book is about Korean sisters on a small island. Does she have to personally be each of those cultural groups to write about them? She notes that she does have a Chinese ancestry. But the bigger question is, why does it matter? As long as she did the research, why does it matter if she has red hair and white skin?

Here is an excerpt from an interview she gave.

And the question See likes best is: Where does a woman who looks like she does—red hair, pale skin—get the right to write novels with titles like "Snow Flower and the Secret Fan" or "Shanghai Girls"?

That is, novels about Chinese people.

"I get challenged every single day," See says. "A woman in line at a book signing said, 'You're not Chinese!' I love that, because I get to talk with people about my family and how much it means to me."

See is only one-eighth Chinese, but she's the great-granddaughter of Fong See, a 19th century entrepreneur who defied racist laws to marry a white woman named Letticie Pruett, own property (including the first Ford purchased by a Chinese person in America), become the patriarch of L.A.'s Chinatown and live to be 100.

"I have 400 relatives in Los Angeles," See says. "A few look like me, most are full Chinese and the rest are in between."

[https://www.sun-sentinel.com/entertainment/events/fl-xpm-2011-06-19-fl-books-lisa-see-20110619-story.html]

As you can see, even famous authors get questioned on what makes them qualified to write stories about characters who may be visibly different from them.

The key is to realize that you will always be questioned because you only have one life to live—your own. Every character you write outside of an autobiography is not you, and therefore you will need to do research as well as use your imagination to put yourself in that character's shoes or socks or flip-flops or boots.

Writing Asian romantic characters can be rewarding and fun as long as you avoid the landmines of common tropes and stereotypes and develop interesting, heroic, and well-rounded or edgy characters that readers love to follow.

The Danger of a Single Story

Several years ago, the writer Chimamanda Ngozi Adichie gave an awesome TED Talk called "The Danger of a Single Story."

https://www.ted.com/talks/chimamanda_ngozi_adichie_the_danger_of_a_single_story

If the only story you knew about a person was that he's a professor, all sorts of stereotypes come in and you use your imagination to fill in the blanks.

Similarly, if the only story you knew about a particular group of people was the single story of their country of origin, again, you have no basis in creating a fully fleshed out image of these people other than the traits of the single definition.

Chimamanda tells about a person who her mother defined as "poor." Because her only story of the person's family was that they were poor, she was shocked to see the beautiful raffia baskets the family produced when she visited.

A single story never does justice to anyone—not a person, or a place, or a nation, or a community.

The more stories we have in our possession, the more we can see the individuality of each person, and the more we can appreciate their humanity.

This is the main reason we need more stories and more representation in our stories.

Our characters show the world that people with Asian faces are individuals worth following, loving, and rooting for. They are not doing stereotyped things centered around their ethnicity. They are doing what regular people do: investigating murders, falling in love, getting kidnapped, working a job, making friends, enemies, and solving problems. They don't wrap themselves around a shroud of ethnicity, nor do they go around imparting Ancient Chinese wisdom, paint tea eggs all day, and throw mahjong tiles at each other.

They simply live, love, work, and play. Yes, they might do things a little differently because of culture, and the food could be different, maybe not. They might listen to rock, rap, country, or techno, or maybe not. And like all of us, they adopt practices from the people around them. So, Dylan Jewell, a white American, makes Mexican hot chocolate but adds a pinch of turmeric to it, and Evie Sanchez, a Filipina, likes hard rock and not hip-hop. That's okay, because everyone is an individual, and people are people everywhere.

Thank you for joining this journey along with me. I look forward to your romances with a diverse cast of characters. Please let me know if I've helped and send me a link to your romance so I can include it as an example in a future edition of this book. Join my online Romance In A Month group to chat with us, a diverse and friendly group of romance writers.

Appendix

My Romances with Asian Leads

- *Knowing Vera* (White H, Filipina h) Zach is a swimmer and Vera is a nurse.
- *Taming Romeo* (Filipino H, Filipina h) Romeo is an actor and Evie is a medical student.
- *Whole Latte Love* (White H, Chinese h) Dylan is a barista and Carina is an investment banking intern.
- *Played by Love* (Korean H, White h) Jaden is a university student and so is Ella.

- *Playing the Rookie* (Korean H, Korean-Filipina h) Jay is a professional baseball player and Jessica is a sports blogger.
- *Claiming Carlos* (Filipino H, Filipina h) Carlos is a cook and Choco is a restaurant owner.
- *Roaring Hot!* (Japanese-Greek-Filipino H, Japanese h) Teo is a motorcycle racer and Amy is an actress.
- *Christmas Lovebirds* (half-Chinese H, White h) Rob is a doctor and Melisa is a kindergarten teacher.
- *Blush of Love* (White H, Chinese h) Matt is a professional football player and Safire is a video game designer.
- *Spring Fling Kitty* (White H, half-Chinese h) Connor is the fire chief and Nadine is an artist.
- *Black Tied* (Chinese demigod H, Chinese human h) Johnny is the son of the kitchen god and Sapphire is a customer greeter at a bank.
- *Jade: Perfect Match* (Chinese H, half-Chinese h) Aiden is a Navy SEAL and Jade is a writer.
- *Playing Fastball* (Chinese H, White h) Timmy is a professional baseball player and Tina is a waitress.

- *Christmas Con* (White H, half-Chinese h) Braden is a bounty hunter and Samantha is a computer programmer.
- *A Christmas Creek Caper* (Chinese H, White h) Brad is the sheriff and Ivy is a decorator.
- *Bad Boys for Hire: Luke* (Chinese H, Chinese h) [TBD]
- *Getting Genie* (Chinese H, Filipina h) [TBD]

My Favorite Asian Romances and Women's Fiction

- *Interim Goddess of Love* by Mina Esguerra
- *Save the Cake* by Stella Torres
- *When Clouds Touch* by Ey Wade
- *Only Uni* by Camy Tang
- *Vintage Love* by Agay Llanera
- *Cover (Story) Girl* by Chris Mariano
- *All is Fair in Blog and War* by Chrissie Peria
- *Finding X* by Miles Tan
- *My Imaginary Ex* by Mina Esguerra
- *The Assignment* by Geraldine Solon
- *Fresh Off the Boat* by Melissa de la Cruz
- *That Kind of Guy* by Mina Esguerra
- *The Lost Flower* by Geraldine Solon
- *China Dolls* by Lisa See

Acknowledgments

So many thanks to authors Joanne Dannon and Jade Kerrion for reading and giving me pointed feedback. I greatly appreciate their perspectives and their willingness to help.

Grateful thanks to my editor, Kimberly Dawn, for her reminders and accurate edits.

I also appreciate author Mina Esguerra for taking many Asian authors under her wing to teach and encourage them to write romance novellas with Asian characters set either in the Philippines or a Western country.

Finally, I truly appreciate my writing group, Romance In A Month, in those formative years when we shared our writing and updates as well as brainstorming and discussion along with the boxed sets we worked on together.

About the Author

Rachelle Ayala is a bestselling author of dramatic romantic suspense and humorous, sexy contemporary romances. Her heroines are feisty and her heroes hot. She writes emotionally challenging stories but believes in the power of love and hope.

Rachelle is the founder of an online writing group, Romance in a Month, an active member of the California Writer's Club, Fremont Chapter, and a volunteer for the World Literary Cafe. She has won the 2015 Angie Ovation Award for *Knowing Vera* as well as the 2015 Readers' Favorite Gold Award for *A Father for Christmas*.

Check out her Reader's Guide at
https://rachelleayala.net/books/
Get a free starter library of eight (8) ebooks at
https://rachelleayala.net/free-books/
Contact Rachelle at
http://smarturl.it/ContactRachelle

NOTES

NOTES

NOTES

NOTES